PLAYING for REAL

PLAYING for REAL

Stories from
Rocky Mountain Rescue

Mark Scott-Nash

The Colorado Mountain Club Press
Golden, Colorado

Playing for Real: *Stories from Rocky Mountain Rescue*

PUBLISHED BY
The Colorado Mountain Club Press

Founded in 1912, The Colorado Mountain Club is the largest outdoor recreation, education, and conservation organization in the Rocky Mountains. Look for our books at your local bookstore or outdoor retailer or contact us at:

710 Tenth Street, #200, Golden, Colorado 80401
303-279-3080, ext. 2
E-mail: cmcpress@cmc.org

Alan Bernhard—design and composition
Scott Vickers—copy editor
Alan Stark—publisher

DISTRIBUTED TO THE BOOK TRADE BY
Mountaineers Books
1001 SW Klickitat Way, Suite 201, Seattle, WA 98134, 800-553-4453

We gratefully acknowledge the financial support of the people of Colorado through the Scientific and Cultural Facilities District of greater metropolitan Denver for our publishing activities.

First Edition

ISBN 10: 0-9760525-6-3
ISBN 13: 978-0-9760525-6-2

Printed in the United States of America

DEDICATED TO

Bill Schorer & Sandra Fish

Contents

Acknowledgments

For their continuing encouragement and ideas, I would like to thank Shelly Scott-Nash, Joe and Caroline Stepanek, Melinda Marquis, Dave Lewis, Tom Hornbein, Walt Fricke, Dave Rearick, Jonathan Hough, Ben Wilson, Ken Baugh, and Ian Baring-Gould.

For editorial ideas, assistance, and contributions, I thank Dan Lack, Dave and April Christensen, James Gallo, Gerry Roach, Paul "Woody" Woodward, Dave Booton, Jon Horne, Tim Cowen, Chuck Demarest, Ted Krieger, Les Sikos, Dan Mottinger, Tim Holden, Steve Poulsen, Bill May, Steve Dundorf, Pawel Osiczko, Jeff and Lisa Sparhawk, Keith Weisinger and Kelly O'Day, Ida Newcomer, Clint Dillard, Pat Libra, "Big" John Snyder, Bijan Tuysserkani, Kevin Wheeler, Jill Yarger, Scott Whitehead, and Gillian Collins.

For his invaluable help in turning this project into a book, I would like to thank Alan Stark.

Special thanks to my old friends Ron and Marybeth Laughery for helping make this book a reality.

Forewords

∾ TOM HORNBEIN

Not long after Willi Unsoeld and I returned from our climb of Everest's West Ridge in 1963, we were invited to present the keynote address at the national meeting of the Mountain Rescue Association. I decided that my contribution to our offering would be to share reflections on the rescuer's motivation to rescue, this based on presumed wisdom derived from my time with the Rocky Mountain Rescue Group (RMR) during its (and my) formative years (1948–1952), as well as some less intense involvement with its Pacific Northwest counterpart, Seattle's Mountain Rescue Council. Both came into existence at about the same time, without awareness of the other, testimony to a remarkable provincialism prevalent at the time.

To provide some spice to my utterances, one of the issues I opted to regale my audience with was the volunteer rescuer who could be heard grumbling about the incompetent idiots who got into trouble, thereby forcing him to put his own life on the line to try to bail them out. One of the common denominators of being involved in this altruistic pursuit was a mix of pleasurable feelings about participating, feelings such as being out in the mountains climbing again (sometimes rescues being the only outlet acceptable to a reluctant partner), helping someone in need, enjoying the camaraderie of kindred spirits, and a touch of challenge and adventure of a more socially acceptable flavor than risking one's life just to climb a mountain. What I thought I had figured out back then was that to rail against the victim's getting himself (or herself) into trouble just didn't make sense, at least for those of us who were there voluntarily. No one was making us do it.

Savoring Mark Scott-Nash's accounts of his personal experiences as a member of RMR is to revisit a not quite forgotten bit of my own past. I came on the rescue scene near RMR's beginning, a starry-eyed, young climber, captivated by the dedication of its founders, some of them alums of the 10th Mountain Division. When I was a 13-year-old growing up in the Midwest, my parents shipped me off to a camp near Estes Park, Colorado. I discovered mountains. Looking back, that discovery proved to be the major pivotal event in my life. All else followed: climbing led to RMR. Learning, then teaching First Aid provoked a change in goals from geology to medicine. Six decades later, my passion for mountains remains undiminished, albeit mellowed by the passing years. My mountain rescue activities have been succeeded by a passion for exploring the mysteries of human adaptation to high altitude. Thus, RMR bears responsibility for catalyzing a wonderful life in medicine and high-altitude physiology, as well as precious relationships born from the same mountain origins.

These tales of sometimes saving lives, sometimes extricating the bodies of those less fortunate, are written with an uncommon sensitivity and sharing of personal feelings that conveys both the passionate commitment and the rewards of mountain rescue work. Mark provides one of the most intimate snapshots of what goes on inside the rescuer's heart and mind that I have encountered.

Although this book is not an official history of RMR, it nicely tells the story of RMR's beginnings in the late 1940s, salted with descriptions of memorable moments that occurred before the author came on the scene about a decade ago. These flashbacks provide continuity and serve as foundation for the events Mark describes.

So, enjoy your journey through this small volume of vividly told tales of one rescuer's experience, some precious history of the Rocky Mountain Rescue Group as it begins its seventh decade, and an endearing tale of what makes a dedicated rescuer tick.

Tom Hornbein
Estes Park, Colorado
January 2007

∾ Gerry Roach

It's about time someone wrote this book! Mark has filled a long-waiting void with stories, history, motivations, and rationale from the Rocky Mountain Rescue Group (RMR)—one of the world's premier organizations dedicated to technical, life-saving rescues on steep mountain terrain. They simply call their often-heroic deeds, "saves." My own experience illustrates why RMR, and this book, are necessary.

Drawn by the soaring slabs above Boulder, Colorado, called the Flatirons, I started climbing at the tender age of thirteen. My first problem was that I knew nothing about climbing, and my second problem was that I had no equipment. A buddy and I just hiked up to the rocks, and I started climbing up the slippery sandstone in my school shoes. Overcoming rising fear of the fatal fall tugging at my cork soles, I survived my first encounters with the sport now glibly summarized as rock climbing. I deepened my problem-laden approach when I got a little equipment and thought that I knew what I was doing. A fourth problem was riding along the whole time—out of fear of being grounded, my buddy and I did not tell our parents what we were doing. No one knew where we were. Clearly, I was on a doomsday spiral. As parents usually do, they figured out what we were doing, and immediately realized our fear of grounding—but at least we were on the ground. As parents often do, they let a period of pining pass, then agreed that we could climb, but that we had to get proper training. That's when RMR entered my life.

I showed up at all the RMR practices, learned the requisite knots, and helped set up complicated systems for lowering litters down vertical cliffs. To prove that they were playing for real, the litters always had a pretend victim in them. RMR literally showed me the ropes. Our riggings grew more ambitious until one day RMR amazed me by creating a tyrolean traverse between two adjacent rock towers. Eschewing gravity, we moved a pretend-victim-laden litter horizontally from summit to summit. Of course, RMR was not in the business of teaching climbing, but I now had a pool of strong partners to go climbing with, and my skills soared. My list of ever more ambitious climbs was always just a foothold ahead of my ever-present fear of what gravity could do. Then, on a fateful day on Castle Rock, my fear surged ahead of my still-youthful foothold.

Three of us ascended Boulder Canyon's famous Cussin' Crack Route on Castle Rock. The granite-slippery, well-named test piece ignored our oaths as it easily consumed our best efforts. Nevertheless, by midday we were above the crux crack and launched on the summit pitch. The leader went up easily at first as I paid out the rope around my waist from my anchored belay position. Then, he moved to the right, went around a corner, and disappeared from sight. We learned later that this is a harder variation of the route. With the rope still moving quietly upward, I assumed that all was well up at the leader's "sharp end of the rope." However, when the leader was just a few feet from the top of the climb, the rope made a hissing sound that I will never forget, and in the next few seconds, all my training zoomed through a final exam.

The leader had only put in one piece of protection, and his fall covered a number of feet that, even today, makes my palms sweat to calculate. Jerked mightily, I maintained my belay position as the rope burned around my waist at a speed shouting the leader's plight—and ours. If I didn't stop the fall, the ensuing jerk would likely pluck the whole team from the impassive rock. As the rope seared through my cotton sweatshirt, I moved my brake hand across in a well-practiced move to increase friction, and simultaneously gripped the rope tighter and tighter with my leather-gloved hands. Playing for real, I executed a perfect dynamic belay, which dispersed the energy of the leader's fall and brought him to a stop—far below the belay stance. I had passed the initial exam, but of course, there was more, since our cries to the leader brought no response.

The fallen leader was presumably badly injured and unconscious. As he was hanging limp on the rope below us, the two of us at the stance knew that we had to move him one way or the other fast, or he would suffocate from the pressure around his waist. Making our choice, we laboriously lifted the leader to a position where we could see him, then finally got him onto the ledge with us. Like the sound of the hissing rope, the sight of my bloody friend coming toward me is forever seared into my memory.

We administered the immediate aid that we could, but knew that we needed outside help. After splitting our resources, I kicked my nearly motion-freezing fear out of sight, took one of our two ropes, and rappelled back down the now even more prophetically named Cussin' Crack. With only a short doubled rope to work with, I had to stop in the middle of the cursed place to rig another anchor as the beat of the mounting minutes pounded inside my skull. Applying my training, I arrived back on the ground after three rappels, ran to the road and flagged down the first car, which drove me to the nearest phone. Grabbing the receiver from its cradle, I dialed my memorized number for the Rocky Mountain Rescue Group. This is the moment that makes it clear why we need RMR.

Help arrived fast. After zooming up the easy side of Castle Rock and rappelling down from above, stabilizing medical expertise was on the ledge with the leader an hour after his fall. The ensuing litter lower was just as we had practiced, except that this time the victim was not pretending. The leader recovered from his injuries and went on to live a happy, healthy life. This RMR "save" occurred a half century ago, long before the era of nuts, cams, cable systems, harnesses, belay devices, webbing, winches, cell phones, or 911 operators. RMR, a volunteer organization, has been quietly executing its saves for more than sixty years under the fuzzy flag of public service. We need this book to explain—and thank—this quiet dedication to a grand cause.

Mark carefully composes RMR's complex, sixty-year history into five chapters that are organized thematically by seasons. Each month has its unique mountaineering hazards, and Mark relates dramatic rescue dramas from all seasons and stations—with all outcomes. Not all missions are saves. Cleverly intertwined with the accounts are explanations of the equipment, techniques, and jargon that RMR uses, how the group completes its missions, and the history of the organization. Throughout, we see the experience, strength, expertise, and passion that RMR volunteers bring into the field for every mission. The group's oft-repeated mantra is, "RMR likes to make rescue boring," which is something only a professional group can do. Better, RMR maintains this readiness year after year and decade after decade. Just as RMR quickly and efficiently rescued my fallen friend in the 1950s, they are ready to save you or me tomorrow. *Playing for Real: Stories from Rocky Mountain Rescue* defines this highly professional group of volunteers.

GERRY ROACH
Mountaineer and Author
Boulder, Colorado
December 2006

∾ JOE STEPANEK

Playing for Real captures the spirit of the Rocky Mountain Rescue Group as fully and as completely as the group strives to protect, serve, and deliver its victims to safety. The group's culture, reflected well in these stories, conveys to all the "essential conscience of RMR."

Like Mark, I, too, went away and then came back; I left the Group Leader position in mid-1970, as my career took my wife Caroline and me to the "poor world" with the U.S. Agency for International Development; and upon my return twenty-five years later, I accepted the RMR position as president. And like Mark and the many other rescuers he describes, I took lessons with me as I left, and returned to offer many from my overseas work, and of course learned even more from the Rescue Group three decades later.

These pages say it all when they are at their most poignant. Tragedy does strike and it hits the rescuer early, and these shocks stay in one's soul for a lifetime. The thrill of the rescue and the beauty of Colorado are appreciated, of course, but these memories do not carry the same weight as one's early glimpse of death's door. As with all rescuers and all emergency service providers, early shocks stay, fixed. For me, they are remembered as a victim's hand resting lightly on a mound of snow, surrounded by broken aluminum high on the Continental Divide; a young boy expiring in our litter at dawn; a hike with parents to witness their son's last rest; and for me the most poignant of all, a stewardess's metal garter belt clip on carbonized remains at the Wichita State plane crash.

Mark describes well the feeling of being "liberated by my pager." In the days before pagers, the midnight phone call created the same alarming, tense, yet liberating feeling. "It felt good" can be said of many rescues—this feeling keeps us going and keeps us coming back to serve strangers and friends alike. RMR's staying power over six decades is an inspiration to its new members and to any volunteer service group.

It is therefore with a great sense of satisfaction that I say that Mark's work captures RMR fully as it savors its sixtieth anniversary—sixty years of service, sixty years without a rescuer fatality. Hundreds of victims, families, and rescuers have much to be thankful for—2007 is a time to say "Well done" and to embrace a well-deserved pat on the back. Sixty years is also a good time for some stocktaking and some expressions of appreciation because six decades are within the memories of families, victims, and rescuers alike.

In an age of much public discussion, criticism even, of our form of government, of public expectation, and of public service, this book provides the reader one glimpse of what one service provider is all about. And this small story is but one of thousands, tens of thousands, that represent well America's nonprofit volunteers, as well as salaried employees, who act in the spirit of self-sacrifice and service. We all have much to make us proud.

Joe Stepanek
President, Rocky Mountain Rescue Group
Boulder, Colorado
December 2006

Autumn

"There are only three sports:
bullfighting, motor racing
and mountaineering;
all the rest are merely games."

ATTRIBUTED TO
ERNEST HEMINGWAY

Pinecliffe

*Rescue equipment
unloaded from a highrailer.*
(Photo courtesy of Jeff Sparhawk collection)

IT WAS A LATE OCTOBER WEEKEND in Boulder, Colorado, a town nestled against the foothills of the great Rocky Mountains. The unseasonably warm temperature evoked the soft mood of summer, broken only by the ubiquitous fiery red and orange of autumnal leaves clinging to trees that cast long shadows in the afternoon sun. The western mountains cut a jagged skyline, drawing the eye down to a complex topography of steep, furrowed slopes thickly covered in green pine trees, interspersed with gigantic brown rock ramparts. The rock formations, facing the city, appear to be the surreal, humongous broken bricks of an unimaginably immense wall torn down and strewn against the mountainside by gigantic beings.

The angle of the clear afternoon sunlight forebode winter's undeniable approach in the outdoor recreation capital of the west, drawing out a multitude of hikers and climbers who knew this was likely their last chance to experience the pleasure of summer warmth for the year. Hikers dispersed into the mountain wilderness along the expansive trail network in Boulder County. The rock climbers scrambled to the numerous cliffs, some famously named The Flatirons and The Naked Edge, and others with more obscure names such as The Achean Pronouncement and Der Zerkle, and countless others unnamed. Beautiful weather in Boulder was also an omen for mountain rescuers; the probability of an accident increased as more people poured into the backcountry.

Tim Cowen was one of the technical rock climbers itching to get onto the rock that day. He set out that morning to climb one of the stark cliffs of western Boulder County. He, his wife, Melissa, and their friends Rob and Lucinda Weingruber and Brad Reeder parked near Pinecliffe, a small mountain town in Coal Creek Canyon in southwestern Boulder County. They started hiking down the trail, which began at a wide turnoff on the southern stretch of Highway 72, locally known as Coal Creek Canyon Road, at 10 A.M. They hiked for forty-five minutes to a remote cliff face above South Boulder Creek.

This was familiar territory for Tim, an accomplished technical climber and mountaineer whose ambition and talents had driven him to summit Mount Everest, the highest mountain on earth. His climb today would be far shorter than an Everest expedition, but technically more extreme. He had climbed their chosen rock route, rated a difficult 5.10c, several times before. This route rating is based on a system ranging from 5.0 (easy, but requires a rope) to 5.15 (about impossible). Climbing routes rated 5.10 or higher, where a letter grade of a–d is appended to the number rating to further distinguish increasing difficulty, require extensive mental and physical strength, and movement training, all of which Tim possessed. The route was a line on a vertical face with skimpy handholds and few good foot placements. His familiarity with the route and technical accomplishments had given him the supreme confidence needed to ascend this route. They unpacked their rope and gear and began the climb.

At approximately 11:30, Tim had reached the crux. Rock climbs are varied in difficulty over their length. On many routes, as on this one, there is one move that is the most difficult called the "crux," which generally equates directly to the published rating. On other routes whose ratings might be described as "sustained," the majority of holds, moves, and features will equate to the published rating. Melissa was belaying Tim from above. "Belaying" is a technique of holding a rope tied to a climbing partner for safety. The belayer controls the rope, taking in or letting out slack as the climber moves himself. The rope runs through a small piece of equipment called a belay device. The belay device is a grip amplifier, and allows the belayer to greatly increase or decrease friction on the rope with an easy movement of the arm. If the climber falls, the belayer will lever the brake end of the rope down against the belay device and body, creating more friction on the rope, and thus slowing and stopping the descent of the climber, thus minimizing the risk of injury or death.

Tim was frustrated as he worked the crux. He was stuck. He could not make a tricky move on the cliff face. He tried several times as his frustration grew. He could feel the slow burn of his forearm muscles sending him a warning: "You will not hold on much longer." This warning grated against his mental state, breaking his focus on the climb. Unknown to the casual observer, climbing requires as much mental focus as physical ability. The climber's mind must focus physical energy and stave off anxiety. As in daily life or work, mental determination can be positively or negatively impacted by sleep, food, practice, etc. Imagine the hypothetical climber not getting the usual cycle of sleep he or she requires. Hesitation forces him to stay in place, wasting strength. He has minutes, possibly only seconds left before the muscles in his forearms burn out and weaken his grip. The mental game of working past the most difficult moves on a climb can more ferociously chip away at one's mental focus, causing a downward spiral of mental and physical exhaustion. If he knows he can climb, he has a shot. If he allows this downward spiral of discouraging thought and muscle strain to take him down, then he will fail and consequently fall; nothing will get him to the top of that climb. Climbers across the globe have in fact asserted that it is the mental game far more than the physical exertion that makes or breaks a successful climb.

Tim could feel the sweat in his palms slowly lubricating his grip on the face. He was hundreds of feet above safe ground, and he knew his life depended on his grip and his rope. There was always his rope, intentionally used as a lifeline. And the rope does its job, when used correctly.

Gripped, Tim could not make the move, finally resigning to the inevitable. He yelled "Take in the slack!" in a wavering voice. Every previous time he was in this situation, he would yell "Watch me!": a non-confusing climbing term that prompts the belayer to prepare for a fall. Possibly because the terrain attenuated his voice, or because she was used to hearing particular terms at certain times, Melissa only heard "Slack!" This is a standard climbing signal to let more rope out so the leader can make a move unhindered by rope drag.

Melissa fed out rope. Neither of them comprehended the situation, but the ingredients of stress and miscommunication were now ominously precipitating a major accident. Tim passed through a doorway from which he could not return. A culmination of unusual events and mistakes pushed him through. He had never hesitated on this route before, he confused his belayer with an unusual phrase, and she executed the diametrically opposite action from what Tim needed. His fingers slipped off and he became immediately airborne. He was startled and alert but not seriously frightened like the feeling you get while crossing a busy intersection; you expect the cars to stop for you but watch them with alert suspicion. Tim had fallen on a rope many times before and immediately thought nothing of his lengthened descent. He anticipated slowing down, but felt an alarming acceleration. Mortal terror grew as the world streaked by. He repeated a mantra to himself as the shock of realization rose into a panic: "stop me ... Stop! ... STOP ME!"

Stopping with a body-crushing impact against the rock, the sound of cracking bone radiated from his back; he buckled forward until his chest impaled on his right knee, shattering his sternum. He collapsed into a blob on the ground and could not breathe; his chest burned without oxygen as he fought to inhale. He had landed in extreme pain on a remote ledge one hundred feet above the valley floor, having fractured five vertebrae, his sternum, pelvis, and ankle. He purportedly never lost consciousness. Melissa, in a state of shock, couldn't register in her mind the urgency of the situation.

Rob and Lucinda were near the ledge and were able to approach Tim first. Rob felt an unidentifiably sick, sinking feeling in his gut; a deluge of horrifying images poured over him all at once as his broken friend lay crumpled and panting but barely animate in front of him. How could this happen on such a beautiful autumn day? Why Tim, the expert who had done so much climbing around the world? Rob and Lucinda struggled to shake off the cognitive dissonance, to accept the terrible reality of their friend's plight.

Brad and Melissa descended to the ledge. They desperately wanted to help, but Tim screamed, "Don't touch me!" as they all attempted in vain to make him more comfortable. They were all in shock, their minds were scattered and in distress as they fumbled about, doing whatever they could think to do for their friend. Tim could not feel his legs. Brad and Rob quickly decided to run out and go for help, understanding they could not deal with this overwhelming situation themselves. But as they descended down the complex valley, they wondered if anyone could possibly get him out of there.

Simply happening upon an injured stranger is cause enough for an emergency response. Everyone will immediately focus all their energy on the rescue task. A certain clarity can lend itself in an emergency when one is detached from the actual patient. On the other hand, sometimes when a friend is involved, anxiety and energy are elevated to a height beyond any experience in life. We can get flustered having to make lifesaving decisions about or for our own loved ones.

Brad and Rob ran back to their car for help. Rob reached his cell phone and dialed 911. He described the accident to the 911 operator, who then paged the volunteer High Country Fire Department based in the mountains above Pinecliffe, the fire-rescue department responsible for the area. They responded immediately and were able to get to the accident site within a half hour.

As they approached the site, they came to the realization that this rescue was far beyond their abilities and training. They needed the help of a mountain rescue group and asked the dispatcher to send out a page for Rocky Mountain Rescue (RMR), which specializes in patient "packaging" and transport when an accident occurs far from an ambulance-accessible road. "Patient Packaging" sounds cold and sterile, I know, but as an organization, RMR takes pride in making their patients as comfortable as possible despite difficult backcountry access, weather, patient injuries, and the duration of evacuations.

Down in Boulder, I was incarcerated in a shopping center on this fine day, itching to get out on a hike or climb, something, anything but looking for a couch to buy. I longed to join my fellow outdoors enthusiasts, but was stuck doing a chore with which I was having poor luck. Having returned to my car with my menial self-appointed task unaccomplished, I felt rather dejected with no sofa to show for my efforts indoors. My spirits were instantly recharged with the familiar ring of my rescue pager. The digital readout displayed the following information:

PRI: 1 INC: FRF021019008878 TYP: MUTUAL AID REQUEST
AD: COAL CREEK AT MM 24 1/2 CTY: GI MAP: W21 LOC:
PINECLIFFE CMT1: REQUESTING SEARCH AND RESCUE 40
YOA MALE FELL APPROX 40 FT CMT2: NO LOWER
EXTREMITY MOVEMENT GILPIN HAS CHOPPER ON
STANDBY TIME: 13:47

Rocky Mountain Rescue was being asked to help with a technical evacuation (or, in rescue lingo, an "evac," a term so ubiquitous in mountain rescue that it is used throughout this book) of a seriously injured forty-year-old male climber. I instantly shifted mental gears. A certain clarity and excitement hits us with the tone of a page. I was already in the southern part of the county, close to Coal Creek Canyon, the best location for accessing this accident. I began to drive up the canyon. In chorus, RMR members all over the county interrupted their yard work, roofing, reading, meals, laundry, or studying to jump in their cars and drive up to a mission. This was the 120th call for Rocky Mountain Rescue for the year.

Thirty minutes from the time I was liberated by my pager, I arrived at the first staging area, a large dirt parking lot bordered by a set of railroad tracks on one side and South Boulder Creek on the other. I parked and hurriedly grabbed my personal mountain rescue gear out of the back of my car: first-aid kit, helmet, harness, climbing equipment, jacket, headlamp, water, food, global positioning system (GPS) receiver, and knife, all prepacked in my backpack. Other rescuers had arrived before me and were already in the field.

There was no access by road; the best way in was a path along the railroad tracks. To help facilitate the rescue, a train master from the railroad company had stopped all trains and provided a "highrailer"—essentially a pickup truck with retractable rail wheels used to transport people and equipment down the line. We were approximately one mile from the accident site. Trains were backed up in Kansas and Nebraska, and interstate rail was halted across a quarter of the United States while we charged into the field to exercise our specialty and ultimately do whatever we could to save Tim's life.

A team of us climbed into the bed of the highrailer. We zoomed down the track and passed through two tunnels. The darkness of the first tunnel was made surreal by the yellow flashing strobe on the roof of the highrailer. With breathless haste we arrived at the field staging area. Our team jumped out and unloaded hundreds of pounds of rescue gear onto the rail line.

We were standing on a wide shelf formed by the rail bed. We took the opportunity to survey the scene; the bed traverses the canyon wall 400 feet above South Boulder Creek. The slope below the rail bed, made of loose rock, scree, and dirt strewn with uprooted pine trees, bushes, and logs, fell steeply down to the creek. I looked across the canyon to the opposite side where I saw another team of RMR rescuers. Already at our patient's side, these rescuers busied themselves with Tim's care and evac. In general, those rescuers who have taken the most immediate leadership roles on scene will push for other medically trained members to get into the field and reach the patient as quickly and safely as possible. All other aspects of an operation with this high medical severity will come second to the medical care of the patient.

He was located several hundred feet up the opposite canyon wall on a narrow ledge, where above and below him loomed hundreds of feet of vertical rock. It was now three o'clock in the afternoon. To execute this or any mission effectively, several steps must occur. The patient must be accessed and his medical condition assessed. This requires skills in both climbing and field medical evaluation and care. As the immediate medical care is provided, other members must devise an evacuation route. These routes can be extremely complex in the mountain environment, requiring specialized skill to allow traversal of cliffs, hillsides, and streams, often in harsh weather. The evacuation gear must be carried into the location where it is needed. The litter must arrive at the patient, and ropes must be set on steep terrain. Ultimately, the patient must be carried out quickly, without exacerbating his injuries or compromising the safety of the rescuers. Scores of rescue team members must coordinate the intricate details of each step to accomplish this gargantuan task. They must fit these pieces together fluidly, modifying and adapting as changes and other circumstances warrant, for the safe and successful evacuation of their patient.

Tim had fallen 40 feet—four stories—onto a ledge jutting out from the wall. Once he realized he would live, the most frightening and worrisome part for Tim was his back injury. "I was immediately aware that I couldn't feel my legs. It was pretty scary," Tim recalls. Melissa had descended to Tim and had been waiting with him. "She was in some denial about how seriously I was injured," Tim continues. "I talked to her later and she said she thought I only had a broken ankle."

As it was impossible to fly or land a helicopter anywhere near him, the only way out was to get Tim to where we had staged the initial response on the railroad tracks, and transport him in the highrailer to an ambulance. Our evacuation route was to lower him down the vertical cliffs to the valley floor, carry him across a stream, and haul him hundreds of feet up steep rock scree. This seemingly impossible feat would require dozens of rescuers in dozens of different roles, specialized equipment, and precision techniques.

Safety lines were fixed to move equipment down and then up the far side of the canyon. A 45-pound litter, a dozen 200-foot ropes, a 20-pound full-body vacuum splint, 40-pound oxygen tanks, a 15-pound medical kit, and several 35-pound packs of anchor equipment trucked over rough, loose, steep terrain on the backs of rescuers already carrying 35-pound packs with personal gear. As the equipment arrived piece by piece at the accident site, Steve Poulsen, a 35-year rescue team member, assembled a belay system to hold and lower the litter.

A litter belay works in a similar way to a climbing belay. Whereas a climbing belay can be expected to hold a thousand-pound load, it is highly unlikely a climber would ever produce this much force in a fall, and may not ever fall and load his belay. A rescue litter belay is expected to have a working strength of several thousand pounds. The anchors and equipment must have a higher tensile strength than regular rock-climbing gear.

The litter was rigged for a vertical evacuation. It was now about 4 P.M., a little more than two hours since RMR was first paged. Rich Farnham and Pat Libra volunteered to be litter bearers and put on their climbing harnesses. They attached themselves to the litter and would guide it down the face, as well as give medical care to Tim during the ride. Tim had been given pain medication as they carefully strapped him securely into the litter. The rigging was complete and double-checked. The gear and lowering techniques would have to work perfectly to get the three of them down safely and quickly. One failure would create a monstrous disaster, likely killing them all. Several rescuers helped Rich and Pat get Tim and the litter to the edge. Steve was running the brakes and called out "On Belay, Stop!"—clear, practiced terminology used to inform Rich and Pat that they were secured and ready to be lowered.

Rich and Pat were suspended eighteen stories above South Boulder Creek. Having spent hundreds of hours practicing and rescuing, Rich and Pat trusted implicitly the systems and those running them. There was an army of support personnel above and below them, watching for any potential problems, and with nothing more than a simple keying of his radio microphone, Rich spoke the words "Down Slow!" and they were over the edge, hanging in free space.

Down, working with *gravity*, is our standard first choice of evacuation route—the surest, quickest way to safety, and conversely, the cause of many of these types of accidents in the first place.

Tim said later, "I remember they said they were going to lower me … The next thing I remember I was looking back up at some faces looking down at me and I'm like, wow, I know where I'm going! I kept saying 'don't drop me;' they must have wanted me to shut up."

In the meantime, I had been overseeing the construction of a haul system to pull Tim and six litter bearers up 400 feet from the creek to the rail line. The system used steel cable instead of rope and would be in place at just the right time. More help arrived in the form of rescuers from the Alpine Rescue Team, our sister team headquartered west of Denver in Evergreen.

Rich and Pat continued their ride down the cliff with Tim. From across the valley we watched them descending the gray, granite rock face. The descent itself took only a few minutes before they were at the creek bed in the depths of the valley. From there, the litter was passed hand over hand across the creek water to the opposite side where another team waited, anticipating an uphaul. Six people picked up the litter and prepared for the hard work of this scree-covered uphaul. Though the litter would be pulled up by the haul system, the litter bearers had to hold the litter with Tim inside off the debris-strewn ground. Pat remained as one of the litter bearers.

The litter and team would be hauled up the slope on 3/16th-inch-diameter steel aircraft cable. Cable is nearly static: it does not stretch noticeably when a load is placed on it, allowing the energy transfer from any given haul system to the distance the litter will move at the end of the line to be much more efficient. On rope, even some "static" ropes, a given haul system will have to haul out stretch in a line before the litter moves. Climbing rope is quite dynamic or bungee-cord–like, a characteristic climbers actually need because the rope stretch will absorb some of the energy generated from a fall, cushioning that climber as he falls. This stretchiness creates problems, though, with an uphaul; the litter can bounce too much if a climbing rope is used. "Static" rope is much better, but still has a bungee effect. Steel cable has no bungee effect and is perfect for this type of system.

The cable was strewn 400 feet down the slope and a 4-to-1 mechanical advantage haul system was built at the top using a rope, pulleys, and a special clamp to attach the haul rope to the cable. The rail track itself was used as an anchor. A team of eight haulers were prepared to pull on the rope.

The haul team was standing by when the radio came to life with "Up Slow!" We started pulling the rope and the litter moved up. Tim was impressed; he thought he was fairly heavy for such a maneuver, but it was a standard technique for RMR. We pulled the team up to the rail line. The litter was detached from the hauling cable and loaded in the back of the highrailer by another team. The highrailer drove down the railroad track with Tim under the care of paramedics.

Minutes later, at about 5 P.M., he was at the wide dirt parking lot and loaded in a helicopter. Tim heard that the helicopter would take him and thought, "Oh shit, I'm not doing very well." He would arrive at the hospital soon after and enter his first surgery. After that he would begin a long journey of recovery, back to the place before his body broke and his life changed forever. Perhaps he will never complete the journey and climb again, but being a climber, I can only speculate, with some certainty mind you, that he will try.

Melissa, back at the parking lot where this nightmarish day began, could do nothing but wait with her thoughts. She and her friends had hiked out with the rescuers. Her thoughts plagued her with emotions of denial, confusion, and guilt. Rich Farnham, a paramedic and technical climber himself, attempted to console her. "Melissa [still] feels a lot of guilt about the whole thing, but it was just an accident and this was something that happened at the wrong time," Tim later told me. "I told her this kind of communication mistake has happened to me, too. And climbing is dangerous; if you climb long enough an accident can happen."

THE FOLLOWING SUMMER a small fund-raiser was organized for the rescue teams who helped with Tim's rescue. A slide show at Neptune's, a local climbing store and hangout, was organized for the event. The slide show featured Tim's expeditions and then a short talk about his rescue and how it was accomplished. Rich and I volunteered to talk about the evacuation for RMR.

Tim was having a very good recovery, though he was still wearing a back brace. He started the show with slides of his climbs. The slides were amazing, with the literal high point being Tim's summiting of Everest. He has an impressive climbing résumé, which includes many accomplishments locally and around the world. His accident was not the result of inexperience or ignorance; it was something that all climbers risk when they go "out on the edge"—a true accident. At the end of his presentation he gave an emotional speech thanking the rescuers for saving his life. His voice was shaking as he struggled through his words, barely containing the strong feelings of gratitude while recalling his near-death experience, and happiness to be alive. A few months later, exactly one year after his accident, Tim was able to trek to Tengboche, a village in Nepal near Mount Everest. It meant everything to him to make the journey out of the dark valley of his traumatic injury and back to the high peaks of his life.

This was my seventy-fourth mission for RMR in four years. A life was saved in a very remote location because of the skill, perseverance, and dedication of a team of mountain rescuers of which I was a part. I was able to use knowledge and experience gained from my rescue training, as well as my outdoor recreational experience to help save a life. We solved a problem requiring difficult medical treatment, extreme physical technique and endurance, intricate technical engineering, and massive organizational coordination.

The after-mission feeling, the release of the tension of accumulated emotions of the initial excitement, apprehension of the unknown, setting up and performing the evac using brute-force labor, sweating side-by-side with your teammates as you struggle and trip on steep, rocky slopes with heavy loads, to the simple relaxation of sitting down on a rock at mission base, resonated in a completeness very few experience. It felt good.

Things don't always resolve this nicely. Sometimes there is no chance of saving a life, and there are absolutely tragic, heartbreaking moments, trials of physical and emotional exhaustion, and nauseating revulsion through which, as mountain rescuers, we suffer and will never forget.

But this mission was a resounding success, allowing me to take part in a large organization that solves the esoteric and always interesting problems of saving lives in the mountains. Rescues give me opportunities that range from simply escaping to the outdoors to the highest rewards for myself—helping save the life of a fellow human being.

Death and
the Beginning

*Climbing accident victim being
packaged by RMR members
in Boulder Canyon.*
(Photo courtesy of Jeff Sparhawk)

IT WAS AUGUST 1988. My wife, Shelly, and I were off-route. We were
attempting to hike to the summit of Mount Sneffels, a Colorado
"Fourteener," one of fifty-four peaks rising to more than 14,000 feet
above sea level. The mountain stands between the small towns of
Ouray and Telluride and is technically easy to climb. No ropes are
required, just hiking and a bit of scrambling (easy climbing requiring
the use of hands as well as feet).

Our inexperience was showing in the fact that we hadn't even
thought of bringing our guidebook, which describes the route in
easy-to-understand details. It was early morning and the sky was
overcast. We wore jackets to stave off the high-altitude chill of the
morning. The clean, cold, and wet smell of the mountain air
impressed on me that we were in a remote corner of nature, far away
from the ordinary environment of civilization.

From across the valley we heard rockfall and then someone
yelling near the top of one of the higher peaks. At first I thought the
noise was just caused by some kids who were hiking up one of the
local peaks to trundle boulders. This scenario didn't seem totally out
of the question. But I was wrong. From our off-route location, we
were actually witnessing a climbing accident on Mount Sneffels. We
continued our hike, ignorant of what we witnessed and unaware of
the serious situation developing.

We continued hiking, realizing that we were off-route but essentially having forgotten what we witnessed earlier. Several hours later,

we saw a helicopter circling low in the area. Eventually we came upon an athletic-looking man carrying a 70-pound steel litter on his back. He was on his way up Mount Sneffels (on the actual route) and asked if I would help him carry his overweight load to where a hiker had broken his leg near the summit. The man was one of the leaders of the local mountain rescue team. The excitement of a real life-and-death, or at least life-and-limb, adventure in the wilderness took hold, and I agreed to help. Shelly decided our previous wandering was enough exercise for her and descended back to the trailhead. I traded off plodding the huge load up the steep scree slope to the summit where the victim was lying on the ground, bundled up in clothing and coats to protect him from the cold.

It was tough work, but we finally made it, and I was able to stand on the summit. More of the mountain rescue team showed up, and I wondered how they would carry this poor guy down a loose, rocky, and awkward slope. It was getting late, and feeling exhausted after hiking all day plus carrying a big load to this summit, I gladly descended, leaving the rest of the work to the mountain rescue team.

For the next few days, I was intrigued and excited to have been able to participate in a rescue. It was a new experience and felt very rewarding, like I really made a difference in someone's life. Being a Colorado native, I grew up around the mountains and loved them. I had some exposure to mountain rescue while attending the University of Colorado in Boulder. During a class session just weeks after starting my freshman year, a professor was called to the rock formations west of Boulder to help a stuck climber. That was interesting, to be called out of class in the middle of the day to rescue a climber. I had never heard of such a thing.

The idea of mountain rescue sounded unique and exciting, and would give me another excuse to get into the mountains. Upon returning to Boulder from our hiking vacation, I looked up the local mountain rescue team, Rocky Mountain Rescue. Their next meeting would be during the first week of September.

I showed up just before the start of the next meeting and joined the crowd. The man running the meeting started talking about recent RMR rescues.

The first "mission," as RMR called their rescues, involved searching for a reported missing party at night somewhere in the mountains west of Boulder. It turned out to be a false alarm. Many people commented about how beautiful it was in the mountains that night, and even though it was a false alarm, it was worth going out to experience the wilderness during a calm, warm darkness under twinkling alpine starlight, when they otherwise would have been sitting at home or doing their normal, perhaps tedious chores of life.

The next mission description was quite different. RMR was called out to rescue a rock climber who had been in a rappelling accident. Rappelling is a technique in which a technical rock climber fastens a rope to an anchor and then uses a friction device attached between the rope and a harness around his waist to descend a cliff. The climber has easy control of his descent rate and is able to speed up and slow down, or even stop with ease. This technique requires extreme care because the climber is relying completely on the integrity of his gear and technique. If something is out of place, an accident can easily become tragic.

This accident happened on the Third Flatiron, a famous rock formation west of Boulder. The climber had rappelled off the end of his rope. This can happen when the rope does not reach the ground because it requires multiple pitches, or several anchor points, to complete. In this case, it was dark and the climber did not notice his rope was short and rappelled through the end of the rope, falling the last 30 feet to the ground. Simply tying a knot in the end of the rope, a commonly used technique, would have prevented this accident.

The mission leader described the victim's injuries. They were horrific.

The climber's pelvis was fractured in three places when he crashed to the earth. This was excruciatingly painful to him as he lay on hard, rocky ground. Every time he tried to roll or shift his position, the sharp, jagged bone ends of his broken pelvis scraped mercilessly on the swollen soft tissue of the internal organs of his lower abdomen. He did not think it was possible to tolerate the pressure of such sharp and searing pain when he moved. He had also punctured his bladder, leaking urine into his abdominal cavity, which added a dull inflammation to the moments when he lay still, removing all hope of comfort. He would lie in this state for hours.

A member of the audience felt woozy and couldn't take any more of the description. He stood up to leave and promptly fainted. That was unexpected and understandable. Never had I seen such a reaction from a verbal description of an injury, but never had an accident seemed so vividly real. The accident victim recovered over time and RMR rescuers had helped save his life, evacuating him out of the mountains using their technical skills and experience. These mission debriefings had spurred a wide range of thoughts, from the enjoyable false-alarm hike to the consequences of a rock-climbing accident and dealing with a critically injured person. It was interesting and far more wide-ranging than any preconceived notions I had about mountain rescue. Unfortunately, events driving my life for the next decade didn't allow me to dedicate the time necessary to train for mountain rescue. But during this decade I gained experience mountaineering in Colorado and around the world. Shelly and I went from climbing in Colorado and the Wyoming Tetons to 6,000-meter peaks in South America and then to the highest peaks in the world, the Himalayas. It was an amazing decade of adventure and learning, with successes and failures in ever-larger expeditions and mountains in the far-reaching and isolated cultures of the earth.

Then, ten years after that initial experience with RMR, I was experiencing déjà vu. It was the autumn of 1998, and Shelly and I were again climbing a Fourteener, Quandary Peak in central Colorado near the ski resort village of Breckenridge. This time we were on-route, exactly where we wanted to be, on the challenging West Ridge. The climbing involved minor scrambling on an exposed rocky rib. As with many alpine rock routes, the ridge is generally solid but contains pockets of loose rock. Care must be taken at all times, constantly checking the stability of each hand- and foothold. We saw several other climbers about a quarter mile ahead strung along the ridge. As we approached the summit I looked down one of the steep, loose couloirs, or large gulleys, running down from the ridgeline and saw the aftermath of another climbing accident.

About one hundred feet below the summit, there were three people kneeling over another person lying face up in the rubble-strewn gully. I decided to descend and help with the situation while Shelly hurried up over the summit to find help. As I approached the accident scene, I was surprised to find two of the people attending the victim were my friends Mary Walker and Tom Jensen. I didn't recognize the third man.

The victim lying on the ground was a severely injured and unconscious woman. The man I did not recognize was her boyfriend, who was in almost a frozen state of shock and disbelief. Mary and Tom had been climbing together about ten minutes ahead of Shelly and me. Mary witnessed the accident. She heard a scream and saw the woman tumbling head over heel down the gulley, coming to rest at the spot where she now lay. Mary has a professional medical background as a nurse anesthetist, and she knew how to keep someone alive. She was administering first aid to the victim with what little medical equipment she had.

To keep the victim's airway open, Mary resorted to using a safety pin to attach the unconscious victim's tongue to her lower lip, pinned directly through the flesh. This was necessary since the victim would be there for hours and there was no other way to guarantee her tongue would not block her airway. The victim was stable and I did what little I could, which mainly involved giving Mary moral support while she monitored the victim's breathing. Meanwhile, someone near the summit called for a rescue using a cell phone.

Hours later, as the sun was sinking and we were becoming afraid we'd be shivering there all night with a critical patient, several air ambulance helicopters showed up. We thought this was a good sign and felt somewhat relieved. They flew in circles around us and then left. There was nothing they could do. We were above 14,000 feet, too high for those particular types of helicopters to hover or land. They also had no landing site or any way to pick up the patient while in the air. The gulley we were in was sloping steeply downward, about 100 feet wide with 20-foot walls on each side. We continued to wait, wondering what would happen next. Our hopes weren't completely dashed; at least something was happening. I tried to assure Mary and Tom that the mountain rescue people would be here soon, but I didn't really know what would happen. The victim was stable but didn't look good. She was turning pale and had irregular breathing. She was going downhill, probably bleeding into her cranium, creating pressure against her brain that was slowly killing her.

Suddenly, a paramedic arrived from above with a large medical kit in a backpack. We breathed a collective sigh of relief that help was here and she would be saved. He scrambled down to us and went to work immediately. When he got a radio call, he quickly keyed the microphone and said one word, "Busy," and continued working. I could hear a flurry of radio traffic coming through the transceiver he wore on his chest. We continued to help as the paramedic inserted an airway tube in the still-unconscious woman.

A few minutes later, another chopper arrived. This one was very different from the last two. It was camouflage green, larger, and much louder. It was a Blackhawk from Fort Carson near Colorado Springs. The Blackhawk is a military helicopter with much more power than the previous air ambulance helicopters and can maneuver at high altitudes. They approached and hovered near us. The sound was a deafening, beating roar. A member of the crew was lowered on a cable winch from the chopper to the ground and detached. The chopper flew off, and the crew member climbed over to us with a military litter, which we quickly unpacked and assembled. We carefully placed the victim on the litter. The crew member then radioed for the chopper to return.

This time the chopper came in and hovered dangerously close, approximately 30 feet above us. We were caught in a stentorian hurricane of flying dust and pebbles, chaos caused by the helicopter's rotor wash. The loading cable came down and I clipped it to the litter attachment. It seemed to take forever to get the cable lined up with the litter in the wild wind, but it probably took only a few seconds. I was in the process of inserting the safety pin for the cable clip when the chopper suddenly pulled out like a giant pterodactyl that had given up on its prey. The pilot probably did this because he felt a rogue wind gust, which is common in the mountains.

My thumb was caught in the cable attachment, but it pulled free immediately and I received only a minor injury. The crew member wasn't as fortunate and got knocked down the mountain about 30 feet. However, he was wearing his full flight crew equipment that consisted of enough protective gear to keep him from getting hurt. Though the lift-off was dangerous and nearly disastrous, the litter was attached and the victim was finally on her way.

Members from Summit County Rescue group soon appeared to help us up the gully and subsequently walked with us down the mountain in the dark. The woman's boyfriend was mostly silent, in mental shock about what had happened and the suddenness of it all. When he spoke, he kept promising he would not let her climb that way again, that he would not climb in dangerous places like that again. That is all he would say.

Mary, Tom, and I walked down together through the cool evening. The forest deepened as we moved further below timberline in the darkness. We talked about this wild experience all the way down. The excitement, horror, stress, and dramatic ending of the rescue was still difficult to fully comprehend. Mary broke down and cried as I hugged her, finally allowing herself a much needed emotional release. She had witnessed the accident and taken care of the victim. We arrived at a dirt road and rode on the Summit County Rescue all-terrain vehicles to the trailhead, where some volunteers had brought food and drinks for everyone. Shelly was waiting there. She had helped coordinate information about where we were and the conditions on the peak at the mission base. It was quite chilly now, but we stood outside and ate voraciously, not having had a good meal since breakfast that morning.

The victim on Quandary Peak had a very severe head injury. Despite heroic efforts, she died a few days after her rescue, never regaining consciousness. I felt profoundly changed by the ordeal. Though I did feel sad for the victim and her survivors, I also felt a certain emotional detachment that I thought would help me be a good rescuer, able to do the job with minimal emotional distraction that could cloud my judgment or decisive decision-making ability. It was a new landscape of excitement, danger, hard work, and skill and emotional challenge. This incident was a better test of whether I could do the job of mountain rescue; I was more involved than I was ten years before.

I was also far more experienced in mountaineering, skills that are required and not really taught by mountain rescue teams. I was inspired; I felt this would probably help make my life more meaningful and was something that fit extremely well with my interests and skills. I wanted to become part of a mountain rescue team. I decided to dedicate the time, energy, and expense to make this happen. Coincidentally, the busiest mountain rescue team in the state was in my back yard. I joined Rocky Mountain Rescue and the adventure began.

Mountain Search and Rescue in Boulder

Vertical evacuation practice in a snowstorm.
(Photo courtesy of Jeff Sparhawk)

SHORTLY AFTER JOINING RMR, I discovered several facts about mountain rescue, also referred to as mountain search and rescue (SAR). The current culture and historical background of the group is the inevitable outcome of a rare combination of mountain location and outdoor recreation-minded population. Few places in the country, or even the world, can claim this unique combination. Locations with fantastically diverse mountain sport opportunities are normally far from large population centers, and vice versa. Boulder is famous, even infamous, for its amalgam of people and place.

Mountain SAR, on the other hand, is also an extraordinarily unique emergency service. It is similar to a fire department in organization and response to emergency events, but quite different in the actual work done. Whereas fire departments are oriented toward urban fire and rescue, mountain SAR groups specialize in wilderness rescue in the mountain environment. Wildland fire teams go into the mountains to control fires, but they are generally large operations with massive amounts of equipment and personnel. Mountain rescue teams tend to be small, light, and quick.

Mountain SAR teams are highly specialized in their training and work. And mountain SAR rescuers do their best, most needed, and difficult work far from the trailhead, the point where all but a few news reporters tend to stop. It is rare to see a rescue in progress on a live news feed. When a rescue happens to be close enough to the edge of the wilderness for a TV news camera to catch, it is a fascinating spectacle. TV news catches maybe 10 percent of RMR's most interesting missions.

Only the few mountainous areas in the country have a need for mountain SAR, Colorado being one. The mountain sport opportunities such as hiking, skiing, backpacking, and ice and rock climbing draw a myriad of people ranging from recreationalists to sport professionals. When these people venture into the mountains, a few run into problems. Within the mountain environment are many hazards that cannot be controlled, only avoided. Many accidents that happen in the mountains are directly caused by a mistake the victim made. Other accidents happen without fault other than being in the wrong place at the wrong time.

Boulder County, Colorado, where RMR does its work, happens to have some of the most varied mountain terrain in the country. The city of Boulder lies at 5,480 feet above sea level, nestled in a valley directly below the foothills of the Rocky Mountains. Within the city of Boulder boundaries, lie three 8,000-foot peaks bordered by colossal crags. The most famous of these crags are The Flatirons. These are sandstone outcroppings that rise several hundred feet above the surrounding hillside. The shape of some of the outcroppings conjure an image of the bottom of a gigantic clothes iron. These rock towers and the surrounding mountains attract hundreds of thousands of visitors each year.

Directly south of The Flatirons lies Eldorado Canyon State Park. This park is less than 10 miles away from the city of Boulder and contains some of the best rock climbing in the country. A route in this canyon called The Naked Edge was once the most difficult rock climb ever completed. Eldorado Canyon, known locally by its abbreviated appellation "Eldo," attracts tens of thousands of visitors each year. On any given summer day, one can go watch rock climbers on the sheer faces of formations that rise directly from the roadside.

West of Boulder are the highlands. The mountains rise higher and higher, eventually rising so high that a large part of their mass lies above timberline. Timberline is an astonishingly well-demarcated "line" where the trees in the mountains will exist below but not above. Below this line lie dense pine and aspen forests, sometimes so dense that off-trail travel is very difficult. Above this line, the trees do not grow at all. The line is actually a narrow transition zone where some krummholz bushes, waist-high thick pine bushes, and smaller trees grow, but it is narrow enough that viewed from a distance, it forms a visually sharp boundary. Timberline is caused by environmental conditions such as lack of oxygen, high wind, and low temperature, which makes it impossible for most vegetation to grow above this altitude. The altitude of timberline increases for southern mountains and decreases for northern mountains. It is at about 11,500 feet in Boulder County. Above timberline the mountains are rocky and barren of most life in the summer. In winter, they appear as beautiful snow-capped peaks.

The western boundary of Boulder County runs through these high peaks and happens to be the Continental Divide. The Continental Divide is an imaginary line that runs north-south across the United States. It demarks where water will flow: On the west side of the Divide, it flows to the Pacific Ocean. On the east side, it flows to the Atlantic. Geography can play tricks as to where this line runs. It does not necessarily follow the highest peaks, but rather the largest obstacles to a particular water flow. However, in general terms it does follow high peaks and ridges. The western edge of Boulder County at the Continental Divide generally rises to between 12,000 and 13,500 feet.

The highest peak in Boulder County is the famous 14,245-foot Longs Peak. Interestingly, it does not lie on the Divide but just to the east. This mountain has an amazing history in itself, attracting thousands of climbers each year from around the country. Other high peaks in Boulder County include many high summits in the Indian Peaks wilderness area. These peaks provide an amazing variety of climbing and backcountry skiing. Though Boulder County can be considered partially urban, one can get to surprisingly remote areas in the western part of the county with only a modest effort.

Finally, there is Boulder city and county open space. Much of this includes the famous "green belt" surrounding the city of Boulder. Open-space terrain varies from flat prairie ground to cliffs and foothills. There are many hiking trails, as well as horse and mountain bike riding opportunities. People from around the county as well as the Denver metropolitan area come to recreate on these open space lands.

When the local, state, and federally managed open-space lands in Boulder County are combined with its large recreation-minded population, an unintended situation arises: the need for mountain rescue. This need first arose immediately after World War II when it was recognized that the future would require an organized response to search and rescue of people who were far from the road. This was the genesis of the Rocky Mountain Rescue Group, one of the longest continually operating volunteer mountain rescue groups in the United States.

When the group was young, it needed to learn how to manage difficult rescue operations. Management of nearly all emergency situations today is driven by the Incident Command System (ICS). It is a regimented organizational structure with well-defined jobs and chain of command. Originally applied to manage large wildfires, ICS has been around since the 1970s. Over time, it has slowly been adopted by various agencies such as local fire departments and sheriff's offices. The federal government stepped up pressure on state and local agencies to adopt the system after the 9/11 disaster, and most emergency agencies now operate more or less within the structure of ICS, including RMR. However, RMR has existed, successfully performing rescues, since long before ICS. RMR has evolved a unique command structure that even today, under the auspices of ICS, allows it to operate efficiently, safely, and effectively.

When someone asks for help in the mountains of Boulder County, the call gets routed through an emergency dispatcher, or 911 operator. If it is determined that a mountain rescue is required, by either the location mentioned or an official on the scene, a radio signal is broadcast-coded for pagers carried by all operational members of RMR, requesting response to the area. Further radio communication with other agencies that may be on the scene, such as sheriff's officers or park rangers, or with the actual reporting party, help further pinpoint what may be confusing descriptions of the accident location.

One rescuer, usually the first or second to arrive at the trailhead or end of the road, goes into the field to locate and assess the scene. A command post is set up around RMR's emergency vehicle, also known as "the truck" or "1970." Team members arrive in waves as they drive from various points around the county, grab their personal gear, and check in with command. As the situation is relayed to command by the initial responders, the mission leader determines what medical and technical equipment is required, when it should go into the field, and who should carry it.

The first rescuer in "flags the route," which usually involves tying red surveying tape on branches and rocks, sort of like a trail of neon bread crumbs. The quickest access is likely to be off-trail, and so the route in is generally not obvious. Teams leave 1970 fully loaded with as much gear as they can carry, including a portable radio so that command can keep track of their whereabouts and make an educated guess as to time of arrival. Rescuers feel a big surge of energy at first as the adrenaline hits, which is a good thing as they attack the initial hard work and move quickly to the scene. At this point the mission appears chaotic and unorganized, with lots of radio chatter and running around. But there is generally only one goal during this stage: to get medical and evac equipment to the victim, and rescuers to the scene.

As rescuers arrive at the scene, they go to work at various tasks. Members with more years of experience generally lead teams to accomplish the most complex work. Medical care is the top priority, but usually involves few rescuers who are paramedics or emergency medical technicians. The rest of the team prepares for the evacuation by assembling the litter, placing anchors for belays, and finding a route down. One person is in charge of the overall site operation and reports to the mission leader at site command. He or she relays ongoing status to the mission leader, requesting more personnel or equipment as needed. If a mission becomes too large for the fielded team to handle, the mission leader will ask for help from neighboring mountain rescue teams. The closest team outside of Boulder is Alpine Rescue Team, based just west of Denver, and they are called first.

Before the evacuation starts, an initial litter team of two to six, based on the type of evacuation, is selected. The litter captain is in charge of this team. If one or more pitches of belays are needed, belay teams consisting of a rope handler and a belayer are formed for the first few belay sites. These teams leapfrog belay duty as the litter moves downhill, providing a rapid, continuous lowering of the litter down a slope. If the evac is longer than a few pitches, fresh litter bearers rotate on to the litter to keep it moving while the previous bearers rest. The mission leader monitors this progress, and at the proper time arranges for an ambulance at the trailhead, or a chopper at a suitable landing zone, to be waiting when the victim shows up. Once the evac starts, this continuous series of events moves the victim as rapidly, safely, and efficiently as possible down the mountain. Even so, it may still take hours, and in rare cases days, to move a victim from the accident site to a hospital.

For large searches, this protocol is somewhat different. Though there is a mission leader, the field personnel are split into many teams of one or more searchers to cover as much ground as possible. For a large search, there are usually several mission leaders hard at work with planning, team deployment, the press, paperwork, and logistical supplies such as transportation, food, and water. These missions may span days or weeks with different personnel rotating in and out of various positions. At any point a search may turn into a rescue, at which time the team remobilizes to the rescue mode described above.

At the end of a mission, all team members report back to mission base. Gear is repacked or restocked in 1970 so that it remains mission-ready at all times, 24/7. The team is then demobilized, and everyone restores their personal gear for the next mission. Some members may remain in the field investigating the cause of an accident, especially rock-climbing accidents. RMR reports its findings as part of its corporate mission to provide safety education to the public.

RMR is an *all* volunteer group; no member is paid. The fact that RMR members are not paid does not make them less than professional, however. In fact, a convincing argument can be made that a volunteer group is more dedicated and skilled than a professional group because the volunteers are motivated by the love of the work and not by money.

The number and variety of missions that RMR has performed over the last sixty years gives the group and its members some of the best expertise in mountain rescue in the country. However, RMR's expertise is not gained by experience alone. The group actively researches equipment and techniques for mountain rescue. This research has been going on for decades and is responsible for many equipment and technique innovations. The design and testing of new types of equipment was far more important decades ago when there wasn't the quality and variety of climbing equipment that exists today.

Boulder Falls

Litter crosses a frozen
Boulder Falls on a cable tyrol.
(Photo courtesy of Jeff Sparhawk)

IT WAS JUST BEFORE 7 P.M. on a brisk Saturday evening and I had just finished dinner and was reflecting on the day spent busy with two rescue missions. The first call for RMR happened in early afternoon. A woman had collapsed on the Mount Sanitas trail, just west of town. Rescuers rendezvoused at the popular Sanitas trailhead located at the top of Mapleton Avenue where it becomes Sunshine Canyon Drive. It was a sweltering fall afternoon. Sweat soaked my shirt as I carried a "bash kit," a 35-pound pack full of anchor equipment, slings, carabiners, and miscellaneous hardware necessary to build anchors and technical rescue systems in the field. The train of rescuers ascended the steep trail to where the victim lay, about a half mile up from the trailhead.

She was conscious but exhausted, and a little embarrassed. She had no other injuries, she had just overexerted her middle-aged body on a hot day. We packaged her up in the litter and evacuated her scree-style straight down the slope to Sunshine Canyon to a waiting ambulance. Even though it wasn't a dire emergency, we performed an RMR trademark quick and efficient evacuation.

After repacking gear into "1970," I returned to my car and drove down Mapleton to town. "1970" is a specially modified four-wheel-drive van that contains rescue gear ready to be deployed into the field. It can transport several rescuers and their personal gear while running "hot," with lights and sirens blazing. It also has all the communication equipment necessary to be a mobile command post. Decked out with its emergency lights and rescue logo, it is a somewhat strange and unique sight within the Subaru- and BMW-saturated Boulder streets. Just as I drove past Pearl Street, my rescue pager beeped to life again. This time we were being called to the Eldora townsite above Nederland in the mountains west of Boulder. There had been an SUV rollover accident far from a paved road. I turned and sped up Boulder Canyon. Details from the radio were sketchy. No one had gotten to the accident site yet. I drove up the canyon, through Nederland, and continued west to Eldora. I arrived at the staging area and went to 1970 to be assigned whatever gear was next on the list to be carried into the field. I was assigned two ropes to carry, only about 25 pounds.

We hiked one mile up Forest Service Road 505, a rough four-wheel-drive track, to the accident site. Though it was hot down in town, up here it was cool and pleasant, and we were able to hike quickly to the accident site. Other gear and some rescuers rode in slow-moving four-wheelers at about the same pace we hiked to the accident.

Before we arrived, the victim had died. Though we had responded quickly, he had sustained fatal injuries as he attempted some maneuver in his SUV. Because he was dead, his body could be driven slowly back down the rough road. This would prevent putting rescuers in harm's way unnecessarily by doing a steep scree evac. Had he been alive, RMR would have taken him down a steep, more direct slope to a waiting helicopter ambulance in the flats below, much more quickly and smoothly than the road could be driven.

A group of us hiked back down the road with Nederland firemen, all carrying equipment back to our respective trucks. I helped repack 1970 and again returned to my car to drive home. I descended the canyon listening to the rescue radio chatter and thinking about the day's events. It was a strange juxtaposition of feelings; we had one save and one death; both missions were fairly easy and not emergencies, but required our full response nevertheless.

I finally arrived at home in the early evening and repacked all my rescue gear. I fixed dinner and was settling down for the night when the pager beeped to life for the third time. We were to respond to Boulder Falls, perhaps the most infamous rescue spot in Boulder County, the scene of many highly technical rescues. I ran out to my car and headed up Boulder Canyon one more time.

Boulder Falls is an easily accessible mountain scenic area popular with tourists. It is a 30-foot-high waterfall in a cove near the road. It is formed by North Boulder Creek flowing down a side canyon before it merges with Middle Boulder Creek to form Boulder Creek in the main canyon just below the falls. It is a popular site due to its easy accessibility and tourist reputation. There is a parking area and an easy walk from the roadside along a maintained trail to the base of the falls. The entire waterfall is visible from the end of the walkway. Unfortunately two hazards attract the unaware spectator beyond the end of the walkway. The first is a steep false trail that appears to lead farther beyond the falls, while the second is the pool at the bottom of the falls.

The water flow through the falls varies with the season, the heaviest flows being in late spring to early summer. When the flow gets heavy, the water is dangerous, and it is deceptively easy to be swept away if you plummet into the water. Victims have left the viewing area and fallen into the rapidly moving water only to be swept down over the rapids and killed, their bodies recovered from the dangerous water later. Though swift streams are a common mountain hazard, RMR does not perform this specific type of rescue, though we support other agencies who perform the actual swift-water recovery.

RMR gets called when people are attracted to the other hazard, climbing the false trail up the steep slope above the observation area. It appears easy to climb, but consists of steep rock slabs covered in loose gravel. Inexperienced persons can easily ascend to a hazardous location and get hurt when they lose their footing or slip. At one time Boulder Falls was one of the most common rescue areas in the county, but in recent years signs have been posted to warn people not to climb the slopes. This has cut down on the number of rescues, but hasn't eliminated them.

This time the victim was far above the falls and the water flow was low. By the time I arrived, RMR was trying to determine whether the victim was above or below "the chockstone," a giant boulder blocking easy access through the canyon, located well above the falls. If the victim was above the chockstone, the best route out would be from Dream Canyon, a completely different approach that would require us to move our staging area several miles up Sugarloaf Road. A hasty team already in the field was searching for the victim. The radio clicked to life and Ted Smith reported, "The victim is below the chockstone." Good, we were in the correct location and would not have to restage. But we still had a highly technical evacuation to perform. We hiked in.

A large group of rescuers climbed up to the victim with, among other equipment, the litter and "bean bag," a full-body vacuum splint that can be fit into the litter beneath the victim, molded to his body shape, pumped free of air and which then becomes a rigid but comfortable support. I grabbed the "cable kit," a pack filled with accessories for setting up a cable support system, and a spool of cable. The geography of the side canyon above Boulder Falls is complex. The slope above the observation area tops out and becomes a shelf. Beyond the shelf the terrain is generally flat but interspersed with boulders. Steep walls rise on the sides of the narrow canyon with the river running down the middle. If the water is high, it is not possible to evacuate a victim in a litter without special techniques.

Numerous evacuations over the decades in the same area have forced RMR to carefully analyze the best, most efficient, and safest way to extract an injured party. It always involves setting up at least one "tyrol" (a tyrolean traverse) and possibly two, depending on the situation. A "tyrol" is a method of transporting a victim across a river or gorge on a highline strung across it. Setting up a tyrol is tricky and can be dangerous. It is highly equipment- and personnel-intensive, requiring dozens of rescuers skilled in the technique. Moving the victim in a litter over a tyrol takes many observers and operators to accomplish safely. RMR is extremely proficient in this technique.

RMR uses its standard 3/16-inch diameter steel cable for its tyrol highlines. I was on my way to set up the bottom end of the main tyrol system. This tyrol would allow us to efficiently move the victim from the upper shelf to the Boulder Falls observation area, from where we could easily carry the victim to the road. I was put in charge of setting up the haul system that allows us to tension the cable and lift the litter and victim up. When the victim was in place, the highline would lift the litter off the shelf. The litter would then travel down the highline to the observation area and then be lowered to the ground, quickly and efficiently bypassing the steep and dangerous terrain above the observation area.

A couple of us worked furiously on haul system setup in the fading light of the day, while several others climbed up to the shelf with cable anchor equipment. Someone threw down a rope from the shelf, and I connected it to the end of a cable spool. The cable was reeled out and up, and its end then connected to the upper anchor. All of this work was performed in tandem with another team in charge of the medical care, packaging, and initial evacuation of the victim. He had a leg injury as a result of falling somewhere near the chockstone. After he was packaged—immobilized, strapped in, and covered with protective equipment in the litter—he was hand-carried for a short but difficult distance down the creekbed toward the shelf. Jim Gallo had been directing the crew carrying the litter as they struggled through the water and boulders by headlamp in the late twilight. If the stream were higher, we would have had to set up a second tyrol to get the victim out of the upper section.

It was now completely dark. Boulder Emergency Squad, a support agency for various emergency situations in Boulder County, was called to help and brought gigantic truck-mounted spotlights to try to light the area. Unfortunately, shining the lights directly up the canyon from the road as we moved down made things worse; it was like driving into the sunrise, blinding you to the nearby terrain. Instead, they directed the lights to the opposite wall of Boulder Canyon. The diffuse reflection helped illuminate our side of the canyon and created a weird spectacle for drivers passing the scene in the canyon.

I could see the evacuation team approaching the tyrol loading area. The tyrol would be somewhat tricky in the dark, so we would use it extra carefully and double-check all systems. A cluster of bobbing headlamps was suddenly visible, and the sound of a mass of people warned of their approach. April Christensen had just run up to the loading area with the "spiders," rigging that would attach the litter to the cable pulleys. Ted Krieger was in charge of the loading station. He carefully rechecked the rigging and made sure the victim was stable and comfortable. He then signaled everything was ready and asked for the status of my station. I said we were ready and waiting. He called, "Up on the highline!"

I directed my team of four haulers. We had a 4-to-1 mechanical advantage hauling system setup and started to pull. We would hold onto the haul rope until signaled to stop. The litter lifted off the ground and was held in place by a "tag line," a separate rope attached to the litter to prevent it from freely sliding down the cable. "Down on the tag line" was the next command. The litter moved down the cable over the edge of the shelf. It was suddenly 50 feet above the ground and steadily lowered down with the tag line to the landing zone. "Down on the highline" was Ted's next command, and the haul team slowly let the tension off the highline as the litter was lowered to the ground. The victim and litter were now on the trail in the hands of yet another team.

The team disconnected the litter and carried it up to the road. The victim was now in an ambulance, heading to the hospital now only minutes away. We broke down our system and packed gear again into 1970. All rescuers were finally out of the field at 11 P.M.

I drove home in the sharp, clear air of this windless autumn night. The stars were twinkling above the high walls of Boulder Canyon as I cruised the canyon turns. Suddenly, the city lights were shining in front of me as I exited the mouth of the canyon. I was tired. I hadn't planned on spending the entire day rescuing people; none of us had. But when called, we responded as we always do, with efficiency and expertise. If necessary, we would respond to yet another page, whether it was in a common rescue area or a completely unknown location, whether it was an emergency to save a life or a body recovery. We would be there when called.

Winter

"We had discovered an accursed country.
We had found the Home of the Blizzard."

DOUGLAS MAWSON
ANTARCTIC EXPLORER

The White Trap

Searching for Justin Colonna in a snowstorm.
(Photo courtesy of Jeff Sparhawk)

ON A RECENT BLAZINGLY BLUE SUMMER AFTERNOON I went on a solo hike up a trail from Rainbow Lakes, a cluster of lakes tucked into the forest north of Nederland, popular with fishermen and car campers. I was doing neither; I was on a quest to find a memorial stone. I strolled up the wide dirt trail surrounded by dense green pine trees in the afternoon heat. After about a half hour of steady hiking, the trees began to thin out and appear stunted and knurled. Soon I could see open meadows lined by thick krummholz bushes and lone trees with twisted trunk patterns and branches pointing east, the direction of the seemingly incessant wind. But today was windless as I continued my hike above timberline to the tundra above.

I was hiking west, up toward the sun, now low on the horizon. I hadn't seen another soul for the last hour as the tundra, abundant just above timberline, was now fading to patches of grassy ground sprinkled throughout large boulder fields. I was in the Rocky Mountains, and here is where the simple yet vastly descriptive name of the range comes from. I arrived at a trail switchback and veered off over the barren, rocky terrain toward the general location of the memorial stone.

I did not know the exact spot; I had to rely on my sketchy memory and some fuzzy photos I took of the area. I searched for about 45 minutes, zig-zagging back and forth, up and down the slope, for a prominent rock shown in one of the photos. I finally found a rock that looked exactly the same as what I remembered. I stepped into the middle of a patch of grass in front of the rock and looked up. As I raised my eyes I immediately saw it, the elusively small engraved memorial stone. It had been placed at the spot by Justin Colonna's family and friends on the spot where his body was found. The small pink marble memorial stone had been there for three years, now almost hidden in lush green grass, anonymous among tens of thousands of grey boulders on a wide, nondescript slope inhospitable to life.

DECEMBER 18, 1999. It was two weeks before the turn of the millennium. The fall semester was over for two University of Colorado students who were excited to be out of class and ready for a winter hike. Justin Colonna and Kevin (not his real name) started early on what was a sunny and relatively warm winter day to climb South Arapaho Peak. South Arapaho is an extremely popular climb in the Indian Peaks Wilderness Area in western Boulder County. The peak is commonly climbed in the summer when weather and hiking conditions are much better. All peaks in Colorado are more difficult in winter, when the day is hours shorter, the air sharply colder, and the distance from your car to the summit longer, sometimes many miles longer as snow closes access roads to trailheads. South Arapaho was no exception.

However, the Indian Peaks had received relatively light snow that winter. Though they could not drive to the summer trailhead six miles from the winter road closure, the sparse ground snow allowed the pair to travel reasonably well without snowshoes, so they left them behind.

Hours later, as they descended from their aborted summit attempt, the two were crouching behind a rock, the only shelter they could find against the freezing, hurricane-force wind. The boulder slowed the wind but did not eliminate it as it backdrafted around the rock and battered their shivering bodies. But there was nowhere else to even consider stopping. And they had to stop, to eat some food and maybe drink a now slushy liquid. The wind pierced their clothing, like leaning against a wall of ice. Their fingers and toes were numb, and their jaws moved sluggishly when talking or eating. Their hair, once soaked with sweat, was now frozen stiff around their hats where it was exposed to the elements. Justin was bone tired. His stomach ached for food but he had trouble eating anything. He looked around, saw nothing but rocky, white openness and wildly blowing snow. They were far from the comfort of a warm beach, a roaring fireplace, or even their car heater. Sitting in the freezing hurricane was too much to tolerate, even behind the large rock. After a nibble of food, they stood up to continue their descent. Kevin descended ahead into the white storm. Justin staggered to his feet.

Nine miles directly south of the Arapaho climbers, Shelly, Scott Papich, and I were wrapping up a day of ice climbing. The weather was fantastic most of the day; the sun was shining and the wind was moderate. But we were well within the protection of the forest on an ice outcropping that forms near Nederland each winter. It was a perfect location to practice for the upcoming winter ice-climbing season, to shake out the equipment and exercise muscles seldom used when not ice climbing.

The sinking sun in the late afternoon brought an end to our enjoyable day of ice climbing. We packed up our ropes and climbing equipment and started our descent over snow-covered boulders through the pine forest below. As we descended in the now chilly weather, I noticed the high peaks north of Nederland were now obscured by thickening clouds. The clouds extended to dim the sun until it cast an eerie light low in the late winter afternoon. The clouds were scattering the sunlight, inducing a phenomenon called flat light. This is a common winter lighting effect in the Colorado mountains. It causes shadows to disappear in daylight and snow-covered ground to visually merge with the white sky. The horizon can literally vanish. Throw in a little snowfall and you have a whiteout. Nothing is visible; everything is a shade of white from the ground to the sky. You are as blind as being in the darkest room where your eye can't detect the difference between being open or closed. You know your eyes are open in a whiteout. The light is part of the blindness, and that makes it more alarming.

We soon arrived at our car and loaded our ice-climbing tools and crampons. The weather was deteriorating. The wind was blowing small snowflakes. My hands and feet were getting numb in the colder air. We were glad to be finished and at the car warming up. We drove off and arrived in Nederland about a half hour later. I stopped at the corner gas station to fuel up and down some hot coffee before the drive home. The sky was now ominously dark. Gigantic wet snowflakes were pelting me as I stood outside my car. Though rapid and exaggerated weather changes are common in Colorado, I was impressed by the rapid change from warm, sunny day to dark and dangerously stormy night. The big mountains to the west were hidden in the gloom. The snow was falling so thickly I could no longer see two blocks down Main Street in Nederland. It was freezing outside and I was freezing in the night air. Though Shelly and I had experienced and even thrived in this kind of weather throughout our mountaineering careers, we were glad to be heading home. This time we had no need to be out in the blizzard.

We drove into Lyons about 45 minutes later. It was 5:20 P.M. when my mountain rescue pager beeped to life. Through the crackling static came the words "Rocky Mountain Rescue: Rescue needed at Fourth of July trailhead. RP [reporting party] reports friend buried in an avalanche." We looked at each other. An avalanche! I immediately turned the car around and drove right back to where we just were, heading into the cold intensity of a winter storm at night in the Colorado mountains.

I turned on my rescue radio. Several rescuers had already reported in. Shelly called in, reporting we would respond as I drove up the South St. Vrain canyon. This canyon is a radio "dead zone"; its high walls and relatively remote location shield it from most radio frequency energy. Two-way radios and cell phones are useless there. We wouldn't pick up any radio traffic until we topped out about 25 minutes later. I was mentally listing what special gear I would need for a rescue in these conditions: winter parka, snowshoes, avalanche beacon, snow shovel, ice axe. All of this gear was stashed in my car and could be unpacked in minutes. Standard gear was already in my backpack: headlamp, first aid kit, food and water. I, like Shelly and every other RMR member, could be ready to head into the field within minutes of arrival.

As my car emerged from the canyon onto the high foothills, radio traffic suddenly became clear. The best information we had was that an avalanche had run somewhere on South Arapaho Peak. There was one survivor who reported the incident. A description of the victim was provided by the RP: light-colored jacket, wind pants, leather boots, warm hat. All appropriate clothing for the conditions. Unfortunately, neither the victim nor the RP was wearing an avalanche beacon. Avalanche beacons are small radio transmitters worn around the body. They are specifically designed to help rescuers find victims buried in snow.

The summer trailhead to South Arapaho Peak is at the end of an unmaintained Forest Service road. This road is six miles long and covered by several feet of snow in the winter. Radio reports indicated a Boulder County snowplow would assist us in getting to the avalanche site. The road would be plowed from the west end of the small community of Eldora to the Fourth of July campground trailhead (a trailhead named after the Fourth of July mine, a long-abandoned gold mine in the vicinity). From there, we would attempt to travel by foot and snowmobile to the accident site.

We soon arrived at the road closure. A caravan of ten rescue vehicles queued up to follow the county snowplow. The rescuers drove slowly up the Forest Service road in blizzard conditions. We finally approached the trailhead and parked, jumped out of the car, and ran to 1970, RMR's emergency vehicle, which was parked at the front end of the road. Ian Baring-Gould was handing out snowshoes and avalanche beacons.

Jon Horne, Steve Poulsen, Jeff Sparhawk, Shelly, and I formed one team and headed up the Arapaho Pass trail to the accident site. We hiked fast into the dark blizzard. This trail parallels the north fork of Middle Boulder Creek and sidehills the east wall of the valley. As we ascended, we could hear the rumbling of rescue snowmobiles well below us. The hiking trail was not designed to take snowmobile traffic and so the machines had to approach from a different direction, paralleling up the valley floor. Every so often a snowmobile headlight would break the darkness as it diffused in the clouds and snow. We could see them 500 feet below us, driving into the gloom. Despite their best efforts, the snowmobiles were unable to find an access to the avalanche site.

We continued up in the black, buffeting blizzard, sweating under our insulating clothing. After about 45 minutes of breaking trail and fighting the wind in the dark, we arrived somewhere below the avalanche site. It was not visible in the blackness. The walls of the canyon rose steeply into the blackness and storm around us. We were keenly aware of the threat of further avalanches and there was a foot of new snow ready to slide. All it needed was a disturbance such as someone walking below a slope holding an unstable mass of heavy white powder ready to cut loose. We couldn't assess the avalanche danger in these conditions.

A beam from a powerful headlamp would only penetrate 20 feet into the gloom. We decided that the danger to rescuers was far too great to go on, and we reported the conditions over the radio. I could feel the disappointment hanging in the turbulent air. We were forced to apply the first rule of mountain rescue: Protect the rescuer, don't become another victim. This dashed the slim hope we had of possibly saving Justin.

Frustrated and hesitant, we finally turned around and made our way down the trail. We immediately reached a group of rescuers lead by Ken Baugh. The RP was with this group. Normally, the RP will not be allowed to help with a rescue, especially if it is a friend or relative. They can be dangerously unpredictable in their behavior in the field, with the potential for greatly exacerbating the rescue problem.

This case was different; the RP insisted on guiding us to the exact location of the avalanche site. This wasn't a bad idea, as it was very difficult to find in the dark blizzard. When he found out we had to turn around and could do nothing that night, he started screaming out his friend's name. He had to be physically restrained from disappearing into the night, searching in vain for his partner. Eventually, he realized the futility and his own exhaustion and turned around to walk down. Our group of 10 rescuers slogged back down the trail. Far down in the valley below, spotlights from 1970 lit up the sky in a giant dome of foggy light.

We returned to the trailhead at 1 A.M. The temperature was far below freezing and the wind was blowing steadily. The tracks we had made earlier were already filling in with freshly fallen snow. As we returned to 1970, we heard Dave Hibl volunteer to remain at the trailhead until morning. Our emergency vehicle would stay in place throughout the night with its spotlights directed at the mountain, hoping to provide an attraction for the remote possibility our victim was somehow able to walk down. Shelly and I and the rest of the team drove off and returned home. We finally arrived at home, falling asleep at 3 A.M.

The avalanche site was in an unnamed couloir, or large gully, on the flank of the 13,397-foot South Arapaho Peak. Couloirs are interesting geographical features to mountaineers. This gulley cut through a cliff band and provided a much easier route up or down the face than the surrounding precipices. Snow tends to be deeper in couloirs, deep enough to fill in irregularities in the ground itself. This makes for a smooth and consistently rising slope, exactly the terrain climbers desire and skiers relish. Above timberline, these gullies catch snow that blows across the alpine tundra otherwise unimpeded. It is the same effect that makes a snow fence work, catching and building snow on its leeward side. The deeper snowpack within the couloir is then protected from the sun by the walls of the couloir, retarding the seasonal snowmelt that occurs in late spring and summer. Couloirs in the Colorado mountains contain snow far into the summer. In some places this snow never completely melts from year to year. Unfortunately, the same characteristics that make couloirs excellent mountaineering routes also make them deadly passages in certain conditions. If the snowpack is not consolidated, they turn into death routes. This happens after a fresh snowfall or during rapid warming in the spring when the top layers of snow avalanche down, sometimes in a giant thundering mass.

The couloir in which the avalanche ran is sometimes used as a fast descent route down South Arapaho Peak, cutting miles of trail hiking. The top of it is at 12,200 feet and it is 700 feet long, which places it entirely above timberline. The average slope of the couloir is about 35 degrees, which is the ideal steepness for avalanches. The angle is shallow enough to allow snow to build without sloughing off as it falls, but steep enough to allow a slab of snow to slide once it has been disturbed. The addition of a foot of new snow essentially created a spring-loaded trap that triggered when Kevin disturbed its balance.

As with most mountain rescues, the rescuers involved must be able to perform their job with very scant information. This is the account that RMR understood a few days after the incident: Justin and Kevin were caught in the storm that Shelly and I witnessed at the ice-climbing area. For us, the storm was fairly mild but building in strength. Justin and Kevin were 3,000 feet higher in an open wilderness. Weather conditions become worse as elevation increases. It is colder, the wind blows faster, and more snow is in the air. The highest peaks in the area are exposed to unimpeded wind. There are no trees to diffuse the wind and snow on the surface.

The environmental conditions for a climber worsen as an ascent takes place. There is a temperature drop of 3.5 degrees Fahrenheit for every thousand feet you ascend. On a nice December day, it might be

30 degrees Fahrenheit when a climber departs from a forested trail-head for the summit of South Arapaho Peak. It would be a frigid 16 degrees on the summit of South Arapaho when they arrive. It is almost constantly windy above timberline in winter on South Arapaho. It turns out that the prevailing wind was blowing downhill with respect to the South Arapaho ascent route, adding significantly to the physical difficulty of the climb. When this wind is combined with low temperature, the "wind chill" effect becomes consequential. Wind chill is the effect due to the combination of wind and cold on exposed skin. This combination chills the skin much faster than if it were cold with no wind. For example, if the wind speed were 30 miles per hour and the temperature 30 degrees Fahrenheit, exposed skin would chill at the same rate as if it were -2 degrees Fahrenheit with no wind.

The winter high-altitude environment also exacerbates normal weakening of the climber's body as the ascent takes place. It is diffi-cult in good conditions to consume enough food and fluid to keep up with the rate at which calories are burned and water is lost during a mountain climb. Climbers tend to eat fewer precious calories and drink less life-sustaining fluid in worse conditions because the act of climbing demands more attention. The diminished partial pressure of oxygen at altitude also takes a heavy toll. Humans will experience a loss of strength and energy above 8,000 feet due to the privation of oxygen. The loss increases as elevation increases. The pair was well over 8,000 feet for their entire climb, so their bodies suffered this con-dition for hours.

Despite what amounted to a hostile environment for life, during that December morning all of these factors were manageable, even for climbers of modest ability. But everything changed as Justin and Kevin ascended higher over the windy, snow-covered slopes. Several hours after starting, the climbers approached Glacier View overlook, a saddle-shaped pass 700 feet below the summit. They had traveled eight miles and ascended 4,000 feet to get to this point. The intensity of the weather between the time they started and this point had ratcheted up to alarming levels. At the Glacier View saddle, the win-ter wind is especially intense as its flow funnels and concentrates through the opening. This, combined with their accumulating exhaustion, caused them to rethink their summit attempt.

The cold wind forced a quick decision to turn around. They were now descending and had immediate physical relief from the difficult ascent, but their problems were growing insidiously. They were now in a whiteout. The flat light and increasing snow were reducing visibility to a few feet. We had simultaneously noticed these conditions while ice climbing several miles south of Justin and Kevin. It was milder for us; it had not started snowing at our lower elevation yet.

Whiteouts are extremely dangerous for mountaineers. A climber must rely on excellent navigation skills to maneuver correctly in a whiteout. This usually means "flying by instruments," having and knowing how to use a compass, GPS receiver, altimeter, and map to determine and stay on the correct route. These skills are not easy to learn or practice, and given the clarity of Colorado weather and obvious trails to follow, few hikers have or ever need these skills. Justin and Kevin needed these skills now—the climbers had walked through an ephemeral doorway unaware, and the door was closing.

They made a decision to descend the couloir shortcut instead of retracing their ascent steps. This would get them down below timberline and out of the brunt of the storm much more quickly. They could "glissade," or slide down using an ice axe for control, the couloir in a few minutes. They would soon be back in the relative shelter of the forest, where the wind and weather would no longer dominate their being. For now, they would stop and eat something, trying to regain some of their energy. They found a large boulder and got behind it, attempting to gain a respite from the wind. This boulder was not large enough to completely block the wind, but was the only choice. They sat and ate and drank far less than they needed because it was too cold to remain there.

After 10 minutes they started down again. Kevin, the stronger of the two, hiked quickly for the couloir. He looked back and saw Justin behind him. He noted that the visibility was low, but he could still see his partner. A few minutes later, Kevin started his glissade down the couloir. He assumed Justin was directly behind him. As he slid into the steeper part of the couloir, the entirety of the snow around him started to move. Within seconds it became a giant mass moving like a gargantuan river. It happened quickly, but Kevin instinctively kept his head above the snow as he was uncontrollably swept down the slope. He came to rest several hundred feet below, sitting upright but buried up to his chest.

Kevin was able to quickly dig himself out and look around. His first thought was to look for Justin. He was nowhere in sight. Kevin

frantically climbed up and down the side of the now-hardened avalanche debris, calling out his partner's name. He heard nothing and
saw no sign of his friend. Kevin recalled that he continued to look for
about 45 minutes before he made a tough decision to give up and get
help. His rush of adrenaline pushed Kevin to run the remaining six
miles down the trail in the fading evening light to an emergency
phone in the small town of Eldora, where he called for help shortly
after 5 P.M. Rocky Mountain Rescue was paged within minutes and
responded with its massive but unsuccessful search in the raging blizzard that night.

The next morning a massive search was started at dawn in the
subsiding but still formidable storm. The chances of being recovered
alive after being buried in avalanche debris drops dramatically after
about 20 minutes. All of the searchers were aware of the unspoken
fact that we were now looking for a body, not a live person. Forty
searchers ascended the valley and arrived at the site in the light of day.
It was exactly as described by Kevin. The searchers probed the debris
pile for most of the day in blizzard conditions, finding nothing. There
were no clues except for the remnants of footprints left by Kevin frantically searching for his friend the day before.

Growing danger of a second avalanche due to new snow deposits
ended the search that day. RMR regrouped and called for extra help.
It was no longer an emergency and the extra people were necessary
for a thorough search. When a search or rescue becomes too large for
one team to handle, which happens occasionally, more help can be
found from other rescue teams in Colorado. This is a mutual aid
effort. Each group knows that, if needed, they can get experienced
help from other volunteer teams around the state.

Dog teams specializing in avalanche search were called, as were
professional ski patrollers experienced in the use of avalanche
charges, small explosive devices used to initiate avalanches. These
charges render the avalanche area safe by setting off anything ready to
go and clearing "hangfire," unstable snow that didn't avalanche with
the initial slide. These explosive devices are very rarely used in the
backcountry but are commonly used in commercial ski areas to keep
them safe from avalanches.

It took time to organize this larger group, and so two days later, a
team of more than sixty searchers went in to look for the body. The
weather was clear, cold, and breezy. The ski patrollers climbed high

along the edges of the zones likely to avalanche if given incentive, and threw their charges like grenades. The rest of the team was in a safe location where they could view the entire slide area. There was a call of "fire in the hole" and a few minutes later we felt the concussion of the explosion. A large avalanche poured down the couloir, doubling the size of the debris pile, which is the mass of snow at the bottom of the avalanche path. Everyone witnessing this avalanche was impressed with the display of what we imagined had happened a few days before.

When the area was declared safe, the probe line, a row of rescuers who methodically probe a slope in a grid pattern, again started at the bottom end of the mass of snow. The entire debris pile was probed up into a steep bottleneck. The bottleneck contained no debris, but it did contain large moats, holes between the rock and snow, where a body could catch. Again, nothing was found.

An avalanche probe line consists of a group of people standing elbow-to-elbow in a straight line along the avalanche debris pile. Rescuers each have a 12-foot-long steel pole, which they sink into the avalanche debris near them. Each time they probe the snow, they feel for any unusual resistance. The line moves up the debris pile in unison until the entire field has been covered. If suspicious resistance is felt with the probe, another person digs down in that area until something is found. Probe lines are not 100-percent accurate. So when RMR found nothing on their first probe line pass through the debris, later missions were scheduled to cover the ground again.

After several excursions, hiking an hour from the trailhead to this couloir and spending an entire day searching, not a single clue was found. No body, no clothing, nothing.

The area surrounding the avalanche couloir was also searched. Though Kevin was certain his partner was behind him, he did not actually witness his friend get buried. We could not rule out that the missing climber was somewhere other than the avalanche debris. As the avalanche debris search continued over the next days and weeks, with no clues found, more people were shifted to searching the surrounding area. Searching over the next few months produced nothing new. This wasn't totally unexpected since potential clues could have been covered by subsequent snowfall in the deepening winter.

As time went on, the location of the missing climber was turning into a frustrating mystery. The avalanche couloir was still considered to be the most likely spot to find the body. Most people felt that the spring thaw would reveal where Justin's body was, but that was months off. I would continue to search the area with other RMR members on our own time, and many hours were spent doing this.

By May the snow on the road had melted enough to drive to the trailhead, shortcutting several miles of over-snow travel that we had been snowshoeing or backcountry skiing to approach the trail during the winter. The couloir was starting to melt somewhat. RMR members made more frequent excursions up to the couloir in easier late-spring conditions, but still nothing was found.

It is unusual but not unheard-of to "lose" avalanche victims for more than one year. It had happened not far to the north in Rocky Mountain National Park under eerily similar conditions. A party of four climbers set out to climb the north couloir on Flat Top Mountain on November 1, 1992. A storm moved in as the group began their climb. About halfway up, two of the climbers decided to turn around and traversed out of the steep couloir to a rock island. Visibility had been deteriorating during the storm.

The two climbers on the rock island felt a "strange wind" and turned to see a glove falling down the couloir. They could not see or make voice contact with their partners and descended to find avalanche debris at the bottom of the couloir. They ran out to the trailhead and notified park rangers. A search effort was initiated in the deteriorating weather, but nothing was found that day. A few days later, after a storm dropped more than two feet of snow, two packs were spotted four hundred feet from the top of the climb, but no other clues were found that winter.

The next summer, searches were conducted as the snow melted. There was unusually deep snow that year that did not completely melt. Nothing was found the entire summer, even though this is a popular summer climb, and many people crossed the area where it was thought the two victims rested. Another winter came and passed. The following spring a camera was found melting out of the snow near the bottom of the couloir. It belonged to one of the victims and soon afterward the bodies were finally recovered, a year and a half after being buried. The strange similarity between this accident and the South Arapahoe avalanche did not escape the RMR rescuers. They were both early season avalanches followed by a big storm.

Knowledge of this history kept the group focused on the avalanche site, even through the beginning of summer, though frustration at the lack of clues was growing.

JUNE 10TH, 2000, was a typical early summer Sunday in Colorado. The weather was beautiful, the summer was young, and the green leaves and grass were still a wonderful novelty after the dry, dead winter. Shelly and I were strolling through downtown Lyons a few blocks from our house. My rescue pager beeped to life at 4:30 P.M. The dispatcher's voice broke the crackling static, "Rocky Mountain Rescue, respond to the Caribou townsite for a recovery." A "recovery" usually means that a body needs to be carried out. The body could be the victim of an accident, or even a suicide. Caribou, an old mining ghost town site above Nederland, was in the area of South Arapaho Peak but not along the route we hiked all last winter in our frustrating search for Justin Colonna. I wondered if he had been found.

We walked back home, jumped in the car, and drove up the canyon to Caribou. We received no new information on the rescue radio as we drove up to the townsite. There are some four-wheel-drive roads in the area that lead toward the avalanche site. We met up with some twenty members at one of the access points. No one seemed to know what the story was, but everyone was assuming it was Justin's body we were going to recover. Curiously, we were not driving toward the avalanche site. In fact, Caribou is more than three miles as the crow flies from the Fourth of July trailhead. We all piled into a few trucks and lumbered up the rough road for an hour-long drive.

Earlier that day, RMR member "Big John" Snyder had decided to go for a solo hike up toward South Arapaho Peak looking for Justin, but from a different starting point. He started from the end of the road that we were now driving up, instead of the much shorter Fourth of July trail. As he hiked, he kept an eye out for anything unusual. At some point far above timberline, he spotted an out-of-place color in the uniform gray rocks about three hundred feet away. He hiked over to it and looked.

What he saw was a male body lying face up on the ground. He was dressed in full winter clothing and appeared to have been there for a while. He was lying in a comfortable spot, almost as if he had just stopped for a nap and never woke up. The only flesh visible was on his face and it was remarkably normal looking. The high and dry mountain air had preserved him quite well.

This body fit the description of Justin Colonna except that he was nowhere near the avalanche couloir. He was over a mile east and seven hundred feet higher than where the avalanche originated. How could that be possible? John called in and reported his location. When the evacuation team arrived, we were certain it was the avalanche victim we had spent so many months searching for. We evacuated the body back down the mountain and left for home at midnight. He was later positively identified as Justin. We had finally found him.

This six-month-long operation turned out to be one of the largest recorded by Rocky Mountain Rescue. There were over 10,000 volunteer hours put into this search. But what had happened? We will never know the exact details. RMR members proposed several theories. These theories were based on the known facts and extensive personal climbing experience of several RMR members who have been in similar conditions. Also taken into account was RMR's far-ranging knowledge of how other victims react in similar conditions and situations.

The victim probably died of hypothermia, which is a critical lowering of body temperature. He was lying in a shallow depression, which would have given him only minor shelter from the wind. He was fully dressed, but not crouched trying to protect himself from the wind. It was as if he was trying to go to sleep. People in a normal state of mind would probably crouch or at least look for a larger rock to hide behind. However, in advanced stages of hypothermia, the mind does not function normally and one might even feel euphoric and totally disengaged from reality. This would credibly explain the position in which the body was found.

Kevin reported that his partner was buried in the same avalanche that caught him, so the rescue team spent most of its time searching the avalanche chute. Kevin was certain that his partner was with him during the avalanche. However, Kevin also reported that the last time he saw his partner was approximately 10 minutes before Kevin started his glissade. Kevin never actually saw his partner start his glissade. Also, Kevin was the more experienced and quite possibly the stronger of the two at the time they headed down. This is supported by Kevin's claim that Justin was not feeling strong at Glacier View saddle, precipitating their decision to turn around.

No one believes that Justin was actually caught in the avalanche. One theory was that Justin witnessed his partner get swept away by the avalanche. This would have frightened him, possibly making him decide to descend another way. He then faced the problem of negotiating "cliff bands," steep escarpments blocking easy passage down. Though the cliff bands are not difficult to climb, they might have appeared impossibly difficult to Justin. His only other choice was to ascend and look for another way down. Not having any knowledge of the area, Justin would have become disoriented in the whiteout and ended up where he was found, having trouble keeping warm in the storm due to his weakened state.

This theory fits Kevin's claim that Justin was just behind him before glissading the couloir. The problem is that Justin would have had to witness the avalanche, nearly impossible in low-visibility conditions. Then, to get to his final resting spot, he would have had to reascend seven hundred feet in the storm and walk over a mile, a lot of energy expenditure for someone who was exhausted.

Perhaps they actually split up after their last meal, higher up on the mountain. Kevin descended ahead into the white storm. Justin staggered to his feet. He followed Kevin, but was too weak to keep up and was colder than he had ever been in his life. Kevin soon faded into the whiteout and before Justin knew it, he had veered from Kevin's track, wandering downhill. His mental fog caused by cold and exhaustion caused him to change course only slightly, to hike away from the wind. There was no sign of Kevin, but he knew he must keep going down and would probably see Kevin soon. His slight course change was amplified over time until he was hopelessly lost in a white, frozen, lifeless wilderness.

An hour later Justin must have realized his situation. He kept staggering down the uneven slope, no sign of trees, bushes, lights, or life. There was no shelter for him to take refuge in, no friendly abandoned cabin. No merciful cave. He felt scared, as if he had been wandering in an alpine wasteland for an eternity. He needed to rest, and for some reason did not feel so cold anymore. With no direction to go, he sat down on a carpet of snow and unwrapped a candy bar. He thought if he just ate the bar he would have the strength to continue. But he was so tired and felt the overwhelming desire to sleep. Maybe he decided to just take a nap so he could continue. He didn't feel any fear now and could not think clearly, so he just lay down. He would finally rest. He never awoke.

Kevin was sure he saw Justin very near the start of his glissade, well below where they last ate together. Kevin was consistently accurate when describing locations on the climb, from the altitude at which the avalanche happened to where there was an icy spot on the approach trail.

The only clear fact is that Kevin and Justin discovered their separation far too late. The coroner determined that the victim probably died at about the same time the page went out for RMR and there was no chance of saving him. By the time he realized their situation, Kevin had no way of knowing where his friend was and could not have done anything for him.

After carrying Justin's body down in the dark by headlamp, we drove home and arrived at 1 A.M. This was the same time we had finished on the first day of the search for Justin. We were tired but collectively relieved to get closure for this mission. Justin's family would later visit his last resting place with several RMR members helping to guide them. They placed the small engraved memorial on the spot where his head lay.

THREE YEARS LATER, in the warm summer breeze, I found it. Its polished face displayed the simple message, "Justin Colonna 1976–1999."

The sun sank below the western horizon as I hiked back across the rocky slope to the trail. There was not another soul around and the mountains were silent. Thirty minutes later I returned to the world of life where tall evergreen trees enveloped me in the cool darkness of a mountain evening.

Genesis

Rocky Mountain Rescue's backpackable, gas-powered cable winch (now retired).
(Photo courtesy of Jeff Sparhawk collection)

Rescue Group Meeting Planned

A meeting has been called of interested citizens and organizations of the city and University for the formation of a "Boulder Rescue Group" in the band room of the high school Monday evening at 7:30 P.M.

John Pederson, city recreation director, will be in charge of the meeting. Boulder county sheriff's officers will be on hand to explain what aid and co-operation the group can give in the event of another mountain tragedy.

—*Boulder Daily Camera* Archive
January 29, 1947

A MOUNTAIN RESCUE GROUP was a revolutionary idea necessitated by an unprecedented cluster of mountaineering accidents and tragedies in the winter of 1946–1947. Volunteer mountain search and rescue groups were unheard-of before this, when accidents were few and far between. Subsequent newspaper notices called for volunteers to meet and bring their ideas about search and rescue. The meeting time of the Rocky Mountain Rescue Group was set for 7:30 P.M., the same time meetings have been held ever since.

A steering committee was formed that consisted of Art Everson (the sheriff), Charles Hutchinson, C.A. Hutchinson Jr., Clinton Duvall, Everett Long, Bruce Snow, Clayton Weaver (Forest Service ranger), Stuart Mace, Art McNair, and John Pederson.

The early days of the "Boulder County Search and Rescue Group" were precarious, but a basic structure was formed under the leadership of Hutchinson (as chairman of the group), Snow (a veteran of the 10th Mountain Division in World War II), and another university professor, Harold Walton. Leroy Holubar, the founder of Holubar Mountaineering (a gear manufacturer), volunteered to look into what kind of gear would be appropriate for rescue. Very soon after the initial meetings in 1947, in response to the desire to gain name recognition, the group adopted the captivating name of Rocky Mountain Rescue and became a university student organization that fall.

THE FOUNDATION of the rock-climbing culture in Boulder began with the first ascent of the Third Flatiron, the most recognizable rock formation on the Front Range. First climbed in 1906 by two brothers, Earl and Floyd Mallard, their ascent enticed others, most of whom were inexperienced in the art of climbing. Between that first climb and World War II, Boulder's resident climbing fanatics helped form three active climbing clubs: the Colorado Mountain Club, the University of Colorado Hiking Club, and the Rocky Mountain Climbers Club.

Along with the members of these organizations, inexperienced would-be climbers drawn to the Flatirons began ascending their routes. They would scramble up these rock formations and, with little experience, often find themselves stuck, unable to continue up or climb down. At the time, when the call for help was heard, an expert climber and resident of Boulder named Ernest Greenman was dispatched by the sheriff to rescue them: a simple solution for a rare event.

At the close of World War II, the then intimate climbing community experienced a dramatic increase. Hundreds of military-trained climbers, many from the famous 10th Mountain Division originally based in Colorado, were released from the service. These climbers retained an inherent desire for the dangers and life-risking activities they faced during the war. Not surprisingly, they flocked to the nation's high peaks with ropes to satisfy these cravings. The possibility for an injured or stranded climber grew based purely on the fact that there were now more climbers. In addition, not all of those who attempted were of sound mind and body, and many didn't have any experience at all.

In 1946, Boulder was horrified by three separate climbing fatalities on the Third Flatiron. Harold Walton, professor and climber who lived in the Chautauqua community near the base of the Flatirons, was recruited to help recover the bodies after these accidents. The city of Boulder, in response to these accidents, erected a sign, warning: "Climbing the Flatirons is extremely hazardous. Do not attempt it without proper guides and suitable equipment." Unfortunately, climbing accidents continued to increase.

December brought another tragedy, this time in a more remote location near the Continental Divide. The University of Colorado Hiking Club had set out on a trip to the Brainard Cabin, a Colorado Mountain Club–owned cabin near Brainard Lake at the foot of the Indian Peaks, west of Boulder.

The Hiking Club had arrived at the cabin on December 1st on a warm sunny day with little sign of the strong west wind that plagues this area in winter. Three of the party decided to attempt a climb on Navajo Peak. Navajo Peak is quite challenging and demands advanced knowledge of mountaineering to ascend in winter. Its 13,409-foot summit requires a steep snow ascent coupled with roped rock climbing, all done in severe cold. The group of three, in attempting this climb, fell into trouble.

Recognizing too late the enormous challenge before them, they retreated. Roped together as they descended the precipitous Navajo snowfield, probably hypothermic and exhausted, one of the climbers in the party slipped and fell. They were plucked off their feet one by one and dragged down the slope. There was nothing to stop them—it was like a horse dragging a rider unexpectedly thrown off the saddle over unforgiving rough ground, adrenaline and pain shooting through their bodies as they flailed, thudding down the slope. They came to rest in an excruciating, bone-crunching crash into the rock scree at the base of the climb.

When they failed to return to the cabin that evening the sheriff was notified and initiated a hasty search, quickly covering the most likely locations. Many volunteers were put to use. Despite all of these resources, no one was found for several days. When the parties were located, two survivors were found about halfway between the Navajo snowfield and Brainard Cabin; one had died at the accident scene.

The condition of both of the survivors was grim; one died in a Boulder hospital the following week. If the victims had been found earlier, it's likely they would have lived. Lake Isabelle, where the two survivors were found, was an obvious place to look early in the search. This underscored the embarrassingly ineffectual organization of the untrained volunteers by inexperienced leaders.

One month later, another mountain tragedy triggered the formation of the Rocky Mountain Rescue Group.

On the stark, cold morning of January 27, 1947, the lifeless body of a three-year-old girl was found curled up under bushes in the mountains west of Boulder. She died of exposure in the harsh winter night, hopelessly lost in a child's nightmare of loneliness, shivering in a scary, dark forest, freezing to death. She lay approximately one mile from the warmth of her bed and protection of her family. For most of the night she was surrounded by an overwhelming army of frantic searchers.

Alice lived with her family in a cabin near the town of Sugarloaf, above Boulder Canyon. The previous afternoon she was with her father, who was working at a mine near their home. As the day progressed and the evening winter chill crept into the air, Alice's father told her to go in and put warmer clothes on. The cabin was visible from their location and Alice was familiar with the area, so her father thought nothing of sending her inside unescorted. Hours later, her father returned to the cabin and discovered she'd never arrived. The family desperately searched for an hour. Their apprehension grew as the sun sank, and they decided to call for help.

Art Everson, Boulder County Sheriff, enlisted a massive response from the surrounding area. "The response was wonderful,... Without any hesitation all those we called agreed to go immediately, and by 10 o'clock last night about one hundred searchers were on the job," said Everson. Unfortunately, as in the Navajo Peak accident, a lack of effective leadership experience and trained personnel hindered the search. Clayton Weaver, a ranger from the National Forest Service, did his best to coordinate the unwieldy effort. It was reported that the weather that night was relatively warm with light snow.

The search was called off at 3 A.M., sadly with no clue as to Alice's whereabouts. The discovery of footprints within five feet of Alice the next morning pierced the hearts of the search team. Perhaps she was unconscious or too scared to respond in the dark gloom to the lifesaving stranger nearby. It was brutally obvious in the wake of this disquieting failure that with better search techniques, Alice would have been found alive.

SPECTACULAR MISSIONS dot RMR's history from those earliest days. On January 21, 1948, a C-47, a twin-engine propeller-driven aircraft 64 feet long with a 95-foot wingspan, took off from Stapleton Airport in Denver en route to Grand Junction. Twenty minutes later the pilot, Fred Snavely, reported strong downdrafts and "unexpected turbulence" as the plane approached the Indian Peaks west of Boulder. Though the pilot did not expect such strong winds, the conditions he encountered are common in winter as storms sweep the mountains west of Boulder.

The copilot, Warren Lungstrom (who with crewman Ross Brown were the only other people aboard), had submitted a flight plan intending to fly at 14,500 feet over the mountains, plenty of clearance. However, the plane did not have enough power to overcome the downdrafts it encountered and slammed into Niwot Ridge just east of the summit of Navajo Peak.

They crashed at 12,900 feet. Ironically, they would have cleared the ridge if they had eked out 50 more feet of altitude. They hit the top of a gulley that is now the most common climbing ascent route up Navajo Peak, aptly named "Airplane Gulley," and described in Gerry Roach's *Colorado's Indian Peaks Wilderness Area* guidebook. The C-47 is not a small airplane and left plenty of wreckage that is strewn throughout the gulley. The still visibly scorched rocks above confirm a fiery crash.

At the time, no one had a clue as to where the plane had crashed. RMR was among the organized groups called to help search for it, receiving much-needed positive publicity for their efforts. Although the wreckage was not found until May, RMR went in to recover the bodies of the crew, and this effort built on their good reputation. According to Bruce Snow, this was in thanks mainly to a man named Dexter "Dex" Brinker, who exhibited strong professional leadership that impressed everyone.

Soon afterward, Snow and Brinker would apply their leadership to forge a more formal organization of the group. Probably the most critical event to propel RMR into the future and strengthen it as a professional organization was the culmination of Snow and Brinker's work to make RMR a "Red Cross First Aid Team." This required the group to have an organizational structure and regular training, two critical core competencies of RMR to this day. Training included practicing techniques that ranged from technical evacuations to efficient search organization. The team was now competent enough to help prevent tragedies like the one suffered by Alice and her family in Sugarloaf.

Charles Hutchinson, a founder of RMR and a University of Colorado (CU) professor, forever tied the group to the university. As a result, many of the initial members were students, giving RMR student organization status. University president Robert Stearns personally visited the offices of RMR in the University Memorial Center (UMC) when they were first opened in the early 1950s. To this day, RMR maintains an office at the UMC and recruits students yearly. They are a constant source of energy and enthusiasm for the group.

An early group leader of RMR and a CU geology student named Tom Hornbein would later go on to become one of RMR's most famous and distinguished alumni. During the time of Tom's tenure in the group, an accident occurred on the Third Flatiron in which a student was injured during a descent.

> "This accident clearly points to the dangers inherent in solo climbing, of climbing on unfamiliar routes, and of climbing without sufficient equipment."
> —Tom Hornbein, Group Leader
> *Boulder Daily Camera* Archive, February 19, 1952

This advice remains pertinent to this day. RMR picks up the bodies of solo climbers on an all-too-regular basis.

Another unique and lasting legacy founded by the early members was equipment innovation. This began with Leroy and Alice Holubar. Leroy was the technical-equipment source for the group from the early days. Alice would design and sew clothing, down sleeping bags, and jackets. These efforts founded the group's reliance on itself for rescue equipment needs and avalanched into the tremendous efforts to design and maintain unique equipment such as the backpackable mechanical cable winch that RMR used for decades to haul litters up over thousands of feet of cliff.

Holubar also founded another Boulder institution, the "mountaineering school." Which school, one may ask, as there are many in existence today. In a real sense, he was the inspiration for all of them. In the spring of 1947, Holubar was persuaded to start a mountaineering school to train RMR members in the art of mountaineering, including technical climbing. This school was taught annually. Since many of the members of RMR were also members of the Colorado Mountain Club (CMC), there was a natural transition to forming a school for both CMC and RMR members.

RMR even went so far as to build a "belay tower," where a weight was mechanically lifted (with a mechanism designed by RMR members) and dropped to simulate a falling climber and test a belayer's skill in stopping the fall. Eventually, the CMC took over both the teaching of the school and the belay tower and started the Boulder Mountaineering School (BMS). This was such a popular school in Boulder that many other schools popped up over the decades, modeled on the same principles.

Because of the drive and innovation of early members such as Hutchinson, Snow, Brinker, Walton, Hornbein, and Holubar, the group had strong foundations in the four critical areas that define RMR culture today: strong leadership and organization, rigorous training, meticulous equipment testing for rescue, and innovative rescue techniques. These were not the only ingredients necessary for a successful mountain rescue group but were by far the most important.

The group incorporated as a nonprofit corporation on September 4, 1951, with Hutchinson, Snow, Brinker, and Hornbein signing on as the original directors. Soon afterwards, RMR became successful and confident enough that "branches" were proposed and started in Leadville, Fort Collins, and Laramie, Wyoming (though none of these "branches" survive today). The RMR group was modeled on the Seattle Rescue Council in the Northwest, which eventually became the Mountain Rescue Association.

Over the next decades, the group became the institution it is today as mountain rescue needs increased. Literally hundreds of people have been members, and the group had its ups and downs, but was never in danger of going out of existence, as it was in the early days.

The Rocky Mountain Rescue Group of Boulder is one of Colorado's most exclusive organizations. It has only 25

regular members—but there's always a waiting list of
about 75.

—*Denver Post* Archive
December 10, 1956

Though the "branch" unit idea failed, RMR still has the distinction of being the progenitor of other mountain rescue groups in Colorado. After RMR was founded, the next organized mountain search and rescue group was formed ten years later, the Arapahoe Rescue Patrol (1957). Alpine Rescue Team was formed in 1959, and many more formed after that. Though each team has unique roots and is fiercely protective of its history, RMR was the de facto model of a successful mountain rescue team for all of them.

An excellent example of this was RMR's instrumental role in the formation of the statewide mountain rescue coordinating group, the Colorado Search and Rescue Board (CSRB). The CSRB is responsible for coordinating statewide mountain rescue resources for large-scale rescues that are beyond the capability of local mountain rescue teams. When a team needs extra manpower it can call the CSRB to activate a statewide call for help. RMR member Chuck Demarest helped to form the CSRB and became its first chairman.

RMR has also taken a leadership role in the development of specialized rescue equipment over the decades. A fine example of this was a unique piece of equipment used on many missions when a long, difficult evacuation was necessary.

A backpackable gas-powered cable winch was developed by RMR in the early 1970s to complement the cable system. This machine could be used to raise or lower a litter, rescuers, and a victim on a single strand of cable. It was painstakingly built in the early 1970s and maintained by RMR members over the years. This winch would save a lot of human power and time and was used extensively for long uphauls. A dramatic example of RMR's cable winch capability came on a mission that happened outside of Boulder County.

On October 10, 1981, a man named Larry Jackson attempted a parachute jump into the Black Canyon of the Gunnison from the rim. The Black Canyon is an extremely deep, narrow canyon located in central Colorado. It has vertical walls rising over 2,000 feet from the Gunnison River below, making it a tempting precipice for so-called BASE jumpers, people who participate in the activity of parachuting from ground-based objects such as **B**uildings, **A**ntennas, **S**pans or bridges, and **E**arth or cliffs, thus the acronym. A video made at the time of the jump shows Larry running toward the edge in an attempt to gain the momentum necessary to carry him away from the canyon wall before opening his parachute. The tape shows that Larry did not make a perfect launch from the rim. When his chute opened, it snagged on a rocky protrusion about halfway down the canyon wall. Larry became the first BASE jumping fatality in the United States.

A woman who was taking pictures of the canyon with a telephoto lens reported that she saw what looked to be a parachute hanging about halfway down the canyon wall. Further investigation confirmed that there was what appeared to be a parachute and body hanging from the wall. A helicopter was used to get a closeup look, just in case it proved to be a hoax. No one who participated in the jump admitted that they witnessed anything, probably due to the fact that this is an illegal activity in what was then part of a national monument (now a national park).

The national monument rangers now had a big problem on their hands. There was a person hanging halfway down a 2,000-foot wall who was either dead or alive and unconscious. They could not use a helicopter to retrieve him because of the proximity to the wall. They needed help and knew about Rocky Mountain Rescue in Boulder. They knew that RMR "was considered to be the best in the state" and asked for their help. Lewis Dahm, lead winch engineer, said that RMR would proceed as if the person were still alive and immediately mobilized their resources. A team would drive down to the Black Canyon that night with equipment, including the cable winch. The team arrived at 11 P.M. and camped on the rim so that they could start working at first daylight.

It was decided to lower a litter with two bearers down to the victim on the wall. A cable winch lowering of this length had never been attempted by RMR before, so the two litter bearers who would normally go down with the litter would also be taking "big-wall" climbing gear with them. This equipment would, in theory, allow the rescuers to climb back up the wall in case the litter system got stuck somehow. The extra gear would increase the load on the system, but was a necessary backup in case something went wrong.

The powered winch lowered the litter, equipment, and rescuers. Steve Poulsen and Walt Fricke were the litter bearers that day. Steve recalls, "I was a little nervous as we descended. Everything was hanging from a 3/16-inch-diameter cable. It looked tiny!" After about an hour, they reached the victim and confirmed that he was dead. They loaded his body into the litter and prepared to be uphauled. As they ascended, problems started to arise. The winch would periodically go into "load limiting" and stop. It was designed to pull up to 1,000 pounds, above which it would not pull. Now that they had a victim, they were dangerously close to this limit. Normally, they would be well below it, but the extra big-wall gear pushed them to the borderline.

RMR cable is cut into 400-foot sections and spooled. They had three cable sections out when they arrived at the victim. These sections are attached with connectors that are larger than the cable itself. At one point, a connector became stuck in a groove. The only solution was to have someone rappel hundreds of feet down on rope and work the connector out of the slot. Eventually this was fixed, and the uphaul continued. After several hours, everyone was on top again. The mission was accomplished.

RMR's cable winch was retired in 2001 after three decades of service due to the problems of maintaining a custom-made complex machine. Human-powered rope hauling systems are now used in conjunction with cable. RMR still uses cable for long uphauls and tyrolean traverses because of its superior quality for these particular applications.

RMR has been active for more than sixty years. The group had wobbly beginnings and it nearly collapsed as an organization in the first years. But these initial trials chiseled out strong, organically grown cultural values that have become the essential conscience of RMR.

A. Christenson

Spring

*"The aircraft was located by the
Rocky Mountain Rescue Group
along the north face of Arapaho Peak
at approximately 1430 the following afternoon."*

NATIONAL TRANSPORTATION SAFETY BOARD
REPORT DEN99FA09

Watershed

*Pilot's body being evacuated
down a snow slope.*
(Photo courtesy of Steve Dundorf)

JUNE 6, 1999. I had recently returned to Boulder from a long climbing stint in the Nepal Himalayas. I was relishing the comforts of modern life after living in a tent at 20,000 feet for the previous eight weeks, suffering the cold, altitude, and lack of electricity, plumbing, and a comfortable bed. However, I was not escaping the outdoors I love, only appreciating my suddenly luxurious existence. I returned to modern life, and returned to mountain rescue. I was on my way to a rescue training session.

I arrived early that morning at "the Cage," a term used by RMR to designate its combined office and equipment storage area. The name is an obscure holdover from a time when rescue equipment was stored in a room with wire mesh walls and door. The name has surprisingly persisted so well that all RMR offices over the last few decades have been referred to as "the Cage" whether they had a jail-like look or not. Originally, the Cage was the storage room, distinct from the "office." The several organizations sharing the Timberline Lounge area of the University Memorial Center had separate offices opening into the lounge. There was also a utility room with plumbing and a stairway down to the storage area, which was partitioned into cages, one for each organization. The RMR office was sometimes in the utility room, other times in the lounge area. Later, the rooms were combined but still referred to as the Cage.

It was a cool, rainy day in Boulder. A storm had lingered for the last few days, making it feel more like winter than late spring. I noticed a buzz of excited activity as I walked into the crowded Cage and removed my wet jacket. I asked what was up, and Bill May responded that there would be no practice today. We had a mission: an airplane was reported missing the night before, and we were going to search for it. The single-engine plane was overdue on a flight from Missouri to Winter Park, Colorado. The flight path took the plane directly over the Indian Peaks in western Boulder County.

My excitement grew as I began to understand our next job. How do you find an airplane in the mountains? This airplane was tiny in comparison to the vast ridges and valleys of the Indian Peaks. It sounded like looking for the proverbial needle in a haystack. However, I knew downed-aircraft locating was a specialty of RMR. The group's past record spoke for itself as one of the most successful ground search teams ever.

RMR goes to great pains to research the best techniques for locating downed aircraft and practices these techniques often until they become second nature. Downed-aircraft location helped form RMR as a rescue group and had become a required skill as scores of small airplanes had crashed along the Continental Divide over the decades. I was still a new member and felt the almost overwhelming excitement to not only be part of this tradition, but to potentially help find an aircraft and possibly save lives.

We learned that radar flight track information, called NTAP (National Track Analysis Program) data, for this airplane was obtained by RMR. This program records the radar tracks of aircraft in the area for the Federal Aviation Administration. Because of the low sampling rate, the data are not accurate enough to pinpoint exactly where a plane might have gone down. It does show the direction of travel and last sampled location, which would give us a starting point for our search. The search area was around North Arapaho Peak, a 13,502-foot mountain on the Continental Divide.

We also heard another story. Craig Skeie heard an odd thing the previous day. He was working in what is known as the Boulder Watershed, an 85,000-acre expanse of city-owned peaks and valleys high in the Indian Peaks. The watershed snowmelt contributes a significant share of the city's water supply. Craig is the caretaker of the man-made reservoirs that catch the runoff. The city of Boulder keeps the watershed closed to the public, so usually there isn't much activity in the area. But that day Craig heard the sound of a small airplane flying very low in the gloom of the clouds. The visibility was poor, and Craig could not see the airplane, but remembered the strange loudness of the engine. It lasted only a minute or two, and he thought no more of it. When RMR called him to ask if he'd noticed anything unusual the day before, he recalled the loud airplane engine. And it was heading in the direction of North Arapaho.

Earlier that morning, a hasty team went into the area of North Arapaho to start their search. They carried with them a specialized radio receiver called an "L-Per," and a custom-designed and built antenna array called a "Yagi." L-Pers are commercially available receivers, but Yagis are designed and constructed by RMR members to be efficient, backpackable antenna systems.

This equipment would help us home in on an Emergency Locator Transmitter (ELT) signal. Nearly all aircraft carry an ELT, a transmitter designed to only switch on in the event of a crash. When turned on, it transmits on a special emergency frequency and acts as a radio beacon to aid in the location of a downed aircraft. ELTs do not always survive a crash, and their batteries limit their useable lifetime to only a few days, perhaps a few hours, after a crash.

The ELT search team had left the Fourth of July trailhead, which leads to North Arapaho Peak, at dawn. They were well into their search as we were being briefed. If they could quickly locate the aircraft, a life might be saved and a massive search avoided.

The plan was to use the fire station in Nederland as the search headquarters. Our team drove from Boulder and rendezvoused at the station to play a waiting game in the rainy weather. Most members would remain at the station until the airplane was found. When it was located, we would hike directly to the wreckage and rescue the survivors or carry the bodies out.

The hasty team had not detected an ELT signal, and the search managers decided to send in more teams to get better coverage of the area. I eagerly volunteered; I couldn't wait to get out there even though the weather high on the mountain looked terrible. Tim Holden also volunteered, and so we prepared our gear to hike in winter-like weather high on North Arapaho. We drove to the Fourth of July trailhead and started our hike at 11 A.M. in the windy, cold, and overcast day. Other teams drove to the east side of the peaks and started searching from the watershed area.

We struggled into deteriorating weather. Forty-five minutes later, as we climbed above timberline, the wind increased to gale force and it was snowing. We were in a June blizzard! This weather was not unusual for the mountains of Colorado in early June, and unfortunately we were caught in it. Tim communicated on his radio and arranged to meet the ELT search team at Arapaho Pass. After two miles and 2,500 feet of climbing, we met the team of Skip Greene, Steve Poulsen, and Chuck Demarest as they descended down a ridge to the pass located at 12,500 feet. They had not detected an ELT signal. There didn't seem to be much more to do at this location, and given the blizzard conditions and lack of visibility, Tim, Skip, and Steve decided to descend back to the trailhead.

Chuck and I were feeling somewhat more energetic and decided to descend Arapaho Glacier, which would take us into the western cirques of the watershed, and continue the search as we hiked east out of the high peaks. I strapped on crampons, metal spikes attached to boots that help to climb in steep snow or ice, and grabbed my ice axe to start the technical descent down steep snow.

We were near the base of Arapaho glacier where we finally got relief from the storm's intensity. Almost as soon as the wind became tolerable, Chuck received a radio message: a team searching from the east side in the watershed received an extremely faint ELT signal. It came from the direction of the northeast flank of North Arapaho Peak. The signal was nearly undetectable, but the eastside team was sure they had something.

Chuck and I were the closest team to the signal source, though we were not near the site. We were directed to go north, up to a plateau at an altitude of 12,500 feet, directly below and east of the summit, and check the signal strength from there. Just then a second report of a weak signal was received pointing in the same direction. We started our ascent.

I began to sweat under my Gore-Tex® shell, a wind- and waterproof outer jacket. It was warmer and the storm was abating quickly as the day wore on. The cloudline was lifting and we could now see everything but the upper 500 feet of the peaks. Ted Krieger was carefully scanning the area with his binoculars from Silver Lake dam, several miles east of the peaks. He suddenly reported "something strange" on the upper slope of North Arapaho, something small that didn't look natural. He radioed this information to Chuck and me.

At the same time, I was cresting the plateau and noticed the same object from much closer. It was definitely not natural. It was right at the visible cloudline, still in a misty fog. It didn't look like the surrounding rock outcroppings, its color was lighter. And it had a more complex shape, elongated and jagged; it seemed to be on top of the snow, not buried in it. It was still hundreds of feet above us. We checked for an ELT signal and detected a weak amplitude in the direction of the strange object.

I broke trail through 24 inches of new snow up the next 500 feet, kicking steps in the steep slope until we finally arrived at what was now obviously wreckage. The ID painted on the side of the fuselage confirmed it was the missing airplane. It was extremely mangled. The engine was about 200 feet above, lodged between a large cliff band and the snow slope below. The plane was drifted in under the new snow. We scraped the snow with our ice axes, trying to expose wreckage and find signs of the pilot. It was obvious that the crash was not survivable, so we were looking for a body.

We dug with our ice axes but made little progress on the mass of snow burying the wreckage. We needed a snow shovel. Chuck had an idea. With a break in the weather, several TV news helicopters were now flying in the vicinity, with reporters getting footage for the evening news in Denver. Chuck radioed one of the choppers and asked the crew members if they wanted to help. They agreed and delivered two snow shovels to us. They couldn't land, so they dropped the shovels from overhead. One of the shovels hit the steep snowslope and slid 500 feet down to the basin below. Gone. The other one stuck in place. I grabbed it and started shoveling.

We alternated in the high altitude with shoveling duties. Soon we had the cockpit dug out. It was a tangled mess of smashed instruments. We found no sign of the pilot or anyone else. He could not possibly have survived; we thought he must have been thrown from the plane on impact. We searched around on the slope and found several large pieces of wreckage—a wheel, a gas tank, a wing—but no pilot. It was getting late and we were exhausted. We confirmed the crash was unsurvivable, so no rescue was necessary. We decided the storm had buried the pilot's body, and that we would recover it after the storm abated and we could regroup. Chuck was able to talk the helicopter crew into giving us a ride out in exchange for an interview. We trudged down to a landing zone and hopped into the waiting chopper, which flew us ten minutes down the valley to the trailhead.

I was ecstatic that I helped find the aircraft, but that was tempered by the tragedy of death and a job not yet finished.

TWO DAYS LATER SPRING HAD RETURNED. It dawned bright blue and warm. This was the day we intended to finish the job of evacuating the pilot's body. A team of Rik Henrikson, Ken Baugh, Adam Fedor, Pat Libra, Steve Poulsen, Jim Gallo, Steve Dundorf, Terry Olsen, and I set out from the Fourth of July trailhead with body-evac equipment. All of the new snow that had fallen during the blizzard was already melted. We hiked up to the Arapaho Glacier overlook on the same trail I had hiked two days before. We clipped on our crampons and descended the now icy-hard Arapaho Glacier to the valley below. We were now in the pristine Boulder Watershed.

We descended to the valley floor and ascended the far side to the plateau as before, circling around to the north side of North Arapaho Peak. As we approached the wreckage-strewn slope, Craig Skeie descended toward us. Craig had approached the slope from down in the valley on a snowmobile. Craig had found the body. "He's up there, not looking good." Craig left, not envying our next job.

The scene was starkly different today. Much more wreckage was visible, mostly small pieces of the plane scattered over the snow. A wing gas tank full of fuel was lying at the bottom of the slope. A wheel, pieces of metal and foam, and a wing were lying there. And then we came upon the pilot's body. It had rolled 800 feet down from the main wreckage and had now melted out of the snow. The crash impact zone was visible above. The plane skipped on the snow up high and then slammed into a rock face. It appeared that the pilot may have seen the rapidly approaching mountains too late, was unable to gain enough altitude, and attempted to turn with little room left.

We were ready to load the body and prepared two body bags. We would put the body in the first bag and then put that bag into a heavier-weight material bag. The body was a mangled mass. It was obviously human but so traumatized that you could easily imagine it was just a large animal carcass. I could see a half-circle of teeth in what was his head, but they were skewed at such an impossible angle that you couldn't tell where his mouth should be. The rest of his body was torn up but relatively intact.

Then I noticed that he was wearing a wedding ring. It struck a chord deep down and changed my vision. This was a human being who was alive a few days ago. He had a family. This connected him with everyone there. And though this was a grotesquely difficult job, he was human and his family needed us to help him.

Our plan was to move the body from its current location to a helicopter landing zone, also called an LZ. Several of us bagged the body. We then loaded it on a "sked," a flexible plastic litter that acts like a sled. It can be towed across flat snow or lowered down steep snow with a rope belay.

We towed the sked about a quarter mile to a steep slope where I hammered in two pickets, specially formed aluminum stakes used as snow anchors. I attached a brake plate and threaded the rope. Rik belayed the sked down while two rescuers guided it to a flat shelf below.

A helicopter would not pick up the body today so we buried it in the snow. We piled most of our evac gear, ropes, sked, and hardware in a separate pile. The helicopter could pick up this as well, which would save us a little energy on our hike out. We set off from the burial site and hiked down the valley where we would eventually meet Craig at his house at the bottom of the watershed.

As time passed on our hike down, our mood lightened. I thought about where we were, a place that most people never see. The watershed valleys were closed to the public in the 1970s, ostensibly to help keep the water clean. And although the area had unmistakable human modification to it, such as Silver Lake reservoir, it was still pristine. A lot of snow cover remained late in spring. There were no signs of trash, no tree carvings, no stacks of rocks piled up by hikers. It was a nearly untouched wilderness in the middle of a heavily used recreation area.

We saw several ice falls in hidden side valleys that towered in giant asymmetric pillars. There were steep, long, snow-filled couloirs that ascended dramatic rock faces. There were aesthetic climbing routes following sharp ridges. Most of these routes have seen few, if any, ascents. The ice climbing here could be some of the best in Boulder County. It was amazing for the mountaineers of the group to witness, like having a brand new valley put right in the center of their well-known climbing playground. And the beauty of the snow-covered forest was astounding. It helped to cleanse our spirits and return us to life.

We were exhausted after ten hours of hiking and the evac. The next day a helicopter picked up the body, our gear, and most of the plane wreckage. Several of us revisited the watershed in the coming days, describing the scene to National Transportation and Safety Board (NTSB) investigators, reporters, and family members who had come to grieve and gain closure by witnessing the wilderness where he died.

Soon after, the team got together for an evening party. Sometime during the beer drinking and music the gathering turned into an emotional decompression therapy session. We all talked about the mission, giving everyone a chance to let off steam in whatever way they needed. Pat Libra expressed the beauty and horror in simple words. "Yeah, that was an amazing mission," he said. "It was difficult to deal with the body, but what a spectacular place to hike. The contrast was incredible." *Difficult:* hard to endure. *Spectacular:* dramatically thrilling and beautiful. *Incredible:* so extraordinary as to seem impossible. We began to understand how this would change us. The dissonance of these powerful emotions that lay at opposite ends of the psychological spectrum and forced together in the small mental container bounded by this mission would sear an indelible image in our psyches forever.

Downed Aircraft!

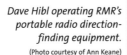

*Dave Hibl operating RMR's
portable radio direction-
finding equipment.*
(Photo courtesy of Ann Keane)

WHEN RESCUE PAGERS FLASH TO LIFE with a call to locate a downed aircraft in the mountains, the search machinery of Rocky Mountain Rescue cranks to full throttle almost instantly. Rescuers prepare for the worst as they listen to the radio for a response location. Mobile radio direction-finding (DF) equipment, located at strategic points throughout the county, is turned on by rescuers who then scan for an emergency locator transmitter (ELT) signal. They relay any information they obtain to a command center where members use mapping technology to begin zeroing in on the crash location. When incoming information is in general agreement as to the crash location, ground teams are scrambled, in sunshine or snowstorm, to a remote and roadless forest or high above timberline on a snow-covered peak. Only a ground team can discover and confirm the exact location and condition of the victims.

Downed-aircraft locating is perhaps the most compelling search work performed by RMR. Not only does it demand large-scale coordination, specialized field skills beyond those normally required for mountain rescue, and dogged persistence, but the media tends to sensationalize this type of disaster. RMR became particularly skilled in locating downed aircraft. From the 1947 disaster in Airplane Gulley (described in the section "Genesis") to the North Arapaho Peak crash, RMR has been one of the busiest search and rescue teams in the country in locating wreckage, rescuing survivors, and evacuating the dead. This unique type of disaster poignantly illustrates the need for an experienced mountain rescue group. Boulder County averages approximately one plane crash per year.

The 1947 wreck put RMR on the map just when civilian aviation was experiencing a rapid increase in business. Airliners were flying more often with more passengers and discovering that bigger planes meant bigger disasters when things went wrong. Many of the regulations that make airline travel today statistically one of the safest modes of transportation did not exist. And when an airplane went down in the remote mountains, finding it was not a simple matter and many times the causes of the crash remained a mystery.

It was almost inevitable that the first large airliner would crash somewhere in the remote western United States, where the unpredictable weather, high peaks, and varying terrain pose unique hazards. It happened on October 6, 1955, on the remote Medicine Bow Peak of southern Wyoming. United Airlines (UAL) flight 409 was carrying 66 people when it slammed nose-first into the side of the mountain at 11,570 feet. At the time, it was the worst air disaster in U.S. history. The cause of the crash was never determined, but speculations were that the pilot was attempting an "unauthorized" shortcut to make up for a late departure, there was an altimeter error, there was pilot error due to carbon monoxide poisoning from a faulty heater, or perhaps engine failure occurred.

According to reports, the crash site was horrific. Body parts were strewn everywhere. It was so disturbing, in fact, that UAL persuaded "U.S. military ground and air forces" to "destroy and bury" the crash site. Reports speculated that the military bombed the site after recovery efforts were complete. However, what actually happened was the face of the mountain was mined with explosives and detonated conventionally in the spring of 1956. RMR member Dave Lewis was one of the witnesses to the event from approximately a mile away. This event was never publicized and access was tightly controlled.

The site was considered so remote and dangerous that the official investigators were not allowed to go to the impact location due to safety concerns. Only rescue workers with mountaineering experience could get to the area and remove the remains of the victims and aircraft wreckage. RMR was asked to assist, along with amateur volunteers from other outdoor clubs such as the Wyoming Outing Club and the Colorado Mountain Club. An improvised cable tram system was set up to remove remains from high on the crash site to a base area, a system that became known as a "Hot Rod Bod Pod." It was essentially a tyrol with a moveable pulley that could raise and lower loads without moving the highline. There were no body bags, so the bodies were crudely roped to the system, wrapped in canvass and evacuated. This is where RMR first acquired knowledge and experience with cable-based evac systems and techniques that would be perfected and used countless times in the following decades.

RMR gained widespread positive publicity for its work in helping with this disaster. There was a disturbing footnote to this disaster; another airliner crashed east of Longmont less than a month later on November 1. This crash killed forty-four people shortly after takeoff from Denver. This time the cause of the crash was found: a bomb destroyed the plane. John Gilbert Graham had purchased several life insurance policies from a vending machine for his mother, Daisie King, who was on her way to Alaska to visit her daughter. Daisie was reportedly nervous about flying due to the recent Medicine Bow crash. She unknowingly carried onto the plane a wrapped Christmas present from Graham, which was a time bomb made of dynamite.

The bomb exploded 20 minutes after takeoff. Graham confessed to the crime and claimed his inspiration was the Medicine Bow disaster, which had received widespread newspaper coverage at the time. Graham had timed the bomb to explode over the same area as the Medicine Bow disaster, which the plane would pass by on its planned route. The plane had a delayed departure in Denver, but the bomb exploded on time, bringing the plane down in Boulder County east of Longmont. Graham was subsequently found guilty of mass murder and executed.

RMR helped with recovery efforts on two other major air disasters. One occurred on June 30, 1956, when two airliners collided over the Grand Canyon, killing all 128 people aboard both planes (again, this was the largest disaster in civil aviation history at the time). Dave Lewis participated in this recovery effort.

He recalled, "The airliners were TWA and UAL. The TWA crash site was near the river and relatively easy to reach. The UAL site was high above the river between bands of vertical cliffs. UAL brought in two RMR members, three Colorado Mountain Club climbers, and a team of Swiss rescuers. Military helicopters were able to land just above the wreckage. The Swiss brought cable gear. UAL procured nylon rope (at RMR's request). Through remarkable teamwork, a cable highline was combined with a rope and pulley hauling system and a horizontal tag line enabling us to raise a load of remains vertically out of a steep gully, then haul it horizontally to the LZ. Later that year, UAL was able to procure the Swiss cable gear for RMR, and we plunged enthusiastically into the cable technology." RMR took the knowledge gleaned from this system back home and improved it, creating a customized version for use on missions in and around Boulder. And changes were made at a national level. This crash became the impetus for the federal law overhauling air traffic control and creating the Federal Aviation Administration.

The other crash occurred on October 2, 1970, when an airplane carrying Wichita State football players crashed near Loveland Pass. There were thirty fatalities, and surprisingly, ten survivors. RMR initially searched the area surrounding the crash site, looking for additional survivors, finding none. The passengers either died instantly, or walked out! A day or two later, RMR evaced a major part of an engine for the investigators. As expected, the 400-pound load ruined our Stokes litter. These were major crashes in which RMR assisted with recovery efforts as part of a greater team.

A new technology for locating downed aircraft emerged. On October 16, 1972, a twin-engine Cessna 310C carrying U.S. congressmen Hale Boggs (House majority leader) and Nick Begich, along with two others, disappeared while flying between Anchorage and Juneau, Alaska, probably near the Chugach mountain range. The largest search in U.S. history was launched by the Coast Guard, Navy, Air Force, and other organizations to locate the plane. The search was called off after thirty-nine days. No clues as to the whereabouts of the wreckage were found or have ever been found. This frustrating failure became the impetus for a federal law mandating ELT use on airplanes to help locate crash sites.

It seemed like a great idea: an automatic radio beacon would trigger when an airplane crashed and searchers could follow a distant signal to the crash site. The reality proved to be not so simple. Though ELT technology improved over time with such techniques as satellite Doppler pinpointing and beacons transmitting GPS coordinates of their locations, radio direction finding requires specialized equipment and techniques that are not easy to perfect, especially in mountainous terrain.

Still, ELTs have proven invaluable. The Civil Air Patrol (CAP) performs air searches, generally in small single-engine planes, for ELT signals and has located numerous wrecks over the decades. As powerful as air search techniques are, they are limited by the simple fact that environmental conditions must be conducive to flight. Storms and limited visibility remove the advantages of air searches because the aircraft cannot fly in those conditions. Also, mountains are notorious for producing unpredictable winds, which make it extremely difficult for small aircraft to fly. Ground search teams are mandatory for mountain searches.

RMR took responsibility to become an ELT ground search team, mainly because of the relatively high rate of plane wrecks in the mountains of Boulder County. RMR has located many aircraft via radio DF-ing (direction finding). Decades of experience and training in mountain environments, as well as the development of custom DF gear, give RMR the distinction of being the best ground search team in the United States. No other team in the country has the background or skill level, especially in the mountains, that RMR has demonstrated.

Two astonishing stories from the first years of radio DF-ing airplane crashes illustrate the bold precedent RMR set for attitude, skill, and urgency in locating downed aircraft and, not surprisingly, survivors.

Buffalo Pass

On December 4, 1978, twenty passengers boarded Rocky Mountain Airways flight 217 in Steamboat Springs, a ski resort town northwest of Denver. Most of the passengers were skiers returning to Denver that evening. The weather was cold with some mixed drizzle and snowfall. The passengers filled the DHC-6 Twin Otter, a dual-engine propeller-driven aircraft, and prepared for takeoff. The plane left the Steamboat airport crewed by pilot Scott Klopfenstein and copilot Gary Coleman, two experienced aviators.

The plane lifted off into the winter darkness at about 7 P.M. that evening and climbed toward the mountain range to the east. Copilot Coleman was at the controls when the first signs of trouble appeared. Flight 217 reported heavy icing that was preventing it from climbing to 13,000 feet, the altitude necessary to safely fly over the pass. They requested a return flight to Steamboat and were immediately given clearance.

Over the next several minutes the situation deteriorated significantly. The pilots continued a broken conversation with Longmont Air Traffic Control Center, but were helpless as the airplane lost altitude. The plane was flying level but sinking alarmingly into the mountainous terrain. At 7:45 P.M., a power glitch was reported in Wyoming when the plane struck a high-tension power line somewhere in northern Colorado. It then slammed into the mountainside. Radio transmissions from the crew indicated they believed they were on the west side of Buffalo Pass, but they had actually flown over the pass and had crashed on the east side.

The Twin Otter held together fairly well during the tumultuous crash into the forest. Everyone survived the initial wreck, but one passenger died within four hours, and pilot Klopfenstein died later. Thirteen passengers suffered serious injuries, including spinal fractures, limb fractures, concussions, severe lacerations, and fractured ribs. However, six passengers received only minor injuries and immediately began to organize and care for the more seriously injured people.

Warm clothing was distributed to ward off the frigid temperatures and the passenger compartment made more comfortable. The pilot was incoherent from a head injury and was taken to the baggage compartment. The copilot was trapped in his seat, surrounded by compressed snow and wreckage. Passengers attempted to make him more comfortable but could not free him.

There happened to be two ELTs on the aircraft, one built-in and one carried in Coleman's baggage. One of the ELTs triggered, and several aircraft in the area reported receiving the signal. The CAP, an organization responsible for nationwide downed-aircraft locating, was notified of the crash via ELT reports at 8:05 P.M., and the Routt County sheriff was notified of the crash very soon afterward, at 8:25 P.M. It was immediately obvious that the crash happened in bad weather and in a remote area, so a statewide call was sent for rescue help. Seven rescue organizations responded with more than 80 people. They were to all rendezvous at Walden, the largest town on the east side of the mountains near Steamboat.

The main contingent of RMR personnel gathered in Boulder while Steve Poulsen and Al Post responded directly toward Walden from their Nederland home. As Steve and Al approached Walden that night, they noticed several people standing on the side of the road with DF equipment. They stopped and introduced themselves as RMR members. The group of people were CAP members attempting to DF the ELT signal from flight 217. They were getting confusing signals. Steve, who was highly trained in DF equipment use, offered to help the apparently confused CAP members.

After some adjustments to the equipment, they agreed the signal was coming from the Buffalo Pass area. They decided to drive toward that area and search for the airplane instead of reporting to the team gathering in Walden. They had detected a signal and had with them DF gear to help pinpoint the source. They became a rogue team, but felt time was of the essence and so didn't report to mission base in Walden—a major break in protocol.

Steve, Al, and two CAP members then drove on following the ELT signal. At one point they noticed a truck towing a "snowcat," a tractor-propelled vehicle designed to move over deep snow. "We flagged down, kind of hijacked, a truck with a snowcat on it," Steve said. The snowcat driver agreed to take the four of them up a power line service road toward Buffalo Pass.

As Steve recalled, "We'd stop every five minutes or so to DF. Fell up to my neck in snow every time I stepped out. The driver knew the area pretty well and followed the service road. It was cold and snowing, about three in the morning. The signal got stronger and stronger as we followed the road, so we kept going.

"By then the RMR truck [with the rest of the RMR contingent] was close enough for radio contact, and I was talking with them on the packset [handheld radio]. They agreed with me and thought I had something. As we drove, I watched the signal get stronger and stronger. At one point it started getting weaker. I told the driver to stop and we opened the door. A voice said 'over here!' They were very happy to see us. I post-holed over to the airplane and called on my packset that we had found it." It was just after 6 A.M. when Steve heard the shouts.

"We had to figure out what we had in terms of injuries," Steve said. The two CAP members were EMTs (emergency medical technicians) and started treating the wounded. "The EMTs with CAP got to work. I admired the medical skill of the EMTs and that rescue is the reason I [eventually] became an EMT myself." Soon two other snowcats and several snowmobiles had gotten to the site. The evacuation of the survivors began, but was not an easy process. It was so cold, Steve recalled, that "intravenous tubing had frozen by the time they got to the cabin [where they staged the victims before transporting them out of the field]."

There was extensive media coverage of the rescue and the saving of 20 lives. Much of the credit went toward the quick action of the rescuers. The official NTSB report on the accident stated:

> Another significant factor in survivability was the prompt organization and dispatch of rescue teams. Although the teams were hampered by poor weather, deep snow, rugged terrain, darkness, and some misunderstanding about the probable location of [flight 217], their perseverance, skill, and determination made an early location of the wreckage possible. This timely location was important because poor weather and darkness prevented any form of air rescue. Consequently, the passengers' and pilots' exposure to subfreezing temperatures and other hazards was reduced to a minimum.

Steve then recalled that "in January the four of us were summoned to the state capitol to receive an award from the governor." But, he added, "It's not really appropriate [to receive an individual award]. I found the airplane, but mountain rescue is a group effort and cannot be accomplished without the team effort: snowcat driver, EMTs, and the evacuation effort. If you remove any of them from that equation, it wouldn't work." Because Steve chose to break with protocol, the survivors were found hours, possibly days, sooner than they would have been otherwise, likely saving lives.

Mount Yale

On Christmas Eve in 1981, a small airplane crashed on Mount Yale, one of the highest peaks in central Colorado. The airplane was carrying a family of five from Dallas to Aspen, where they had planned a ski vacation. The family's father was the pilot, Gary Meeks. He was inexperienced in mountain flying and ran into rough weather. His plane was not powerful enough to overcome a strong, storm-driven wind flowing over the Continental Divide, and thus was unable to climb high enough to clear the final mountain range surrounding the Aspen valley. He crash-landed on Mount Yale. Everyone survived, but some of his family sustained injuries, including a head injury, a broken back, and a dislocated shoulder.

When the shock had faded, they started to examine their dire predicament. They knew they were in the central mountain wilderness of Colorado, but none realized how very isolated they actually were. The shortest distance to a road, which they had no way of knowing about, was five and a half miles. That may not seem so far, but traversing that distance would require plowing up and down over a mountainous, forest-filled land covered with chest-deep snow. The nearest town was Buena Vista, approximately 10 miles from the crash site. It was not possible for any of them to hike out for help; they might as well have been on the North Pole, for their only hope was to have someone find them.

And that prospect was dim. The airplane was painted almost completely white, making it extremely difficult to spot the wreckage in the many square miles of snow-covered forest. Meeks had also made a critical mistake: he never filed a flight plan. A flight plan is a declaration of where a pilot intends to fly. If the plane is overdue, the flight plan triggers a search and is used to help locate the missing aircraft. Flight plans for small aircraft are highly recommended though not required, and Meeks did not file one.

The day following the crash, Meeks decided to try to walk out for help. This bad decision was probably a desperate last attempt to save his family and himself. He was critically unprepared to make this difficult journey even if he knew where he was. Meeks used his aeronautical charts but thought he was in a valley 30 miles north of their actual crash site. Wearing only cowboy boots, jeans, a leather jacket, and gloves, he set out. He broke trail through the deep powder with his son for a quarter mile before sending his son back. He was never seen alive again.

When the sun set on the shortest days of the year on the east slopes of Mount Yale, it was dark by 4:30 P.M. They were now in a freezing winter storm, high in the remote Colorado mountains, and two of them had very serious injuries. No one heard their desperate radio transmissions for help, and because of the lack of a flight plan, no one even knew an airplane was missing. It seemed everything went wrong in this horrific disaster, which had started as a fun Aspen skiing vacation, and the family was facing a slow, tortuous end. But their tide of ill fortune started to turn because their ELT was operational. It had triggered on impact and was working as designed, broadcasting its continuous radio signal.

Three days after the crash, an airline crew monitoring the emergency ELT frequency detected a signal and reported it to air traffic control. They heard the eerie rise and fall of the signal as they flew over the Collegiate Peaks of Colorado where Mount Yale is located. But that was as close as they could pinpoint it. The Civil Air Patrol was dispatched and began a mission to find the ELT.

A mission was launched, but the CAP mission leader was skeptical. No airplane was reported missing, which was nearly always the case for previous searches. And CAP had chased rogue ELT signals before. An ELT is a self-contained device about the size of a milk carton. It could easily be carried by someone and accidentally, or even mischievously, triggered. Even if the signals came from a crashed airplane, would there be any survivors in such an environment? Nevertheless, flights were made around the area and the signal confirmed.

The CAP uses small aircraft equipped with radio DF equipment as its primary search tool. The DF equipment basically shows radio signal strength and direction. The closer the DF receiver is to the transmitter, the stronger the signal becomes. Theoretically, one can simply follow the indicated direction and watch as the signal strength increases until the ELT is found.

However, in practice it is rarely this easy to find an ELT in the mountains. The violence of a wreck can rip the ELT from its antenna connection, reducing the signal power and making it difficult to detect at all. When an ELT does produce a signal, it may only last a couple of days before the battery is drained.

When an ELT signal is present, its radio waves will reflect off of rock and cliff faces, and diffract over ridges, causing DF readings that are confusing. As an analogy, imagine using a telescope (your DF gear) to locate a distant signal campfire at night in the mountains (the ELT signal). And in the place of rock faces and cliffs, these mountains have mirrors facing various directions. As you scan the terrain with your telescope, you see several spots of light of varying intensity made by the reflections from the mirrors. One of the spots may be the fire, but they all look similar. Some spots are brighter and some dimmer. An ELT signal and DF gear sees a similar picture, making the actual location difficult to decipher.

Because of ongoing stormy weather over the mountains, CAP was unable to fly its small planes close to the signal source and could not get a fix on the ELT. It was incorrectly located on Mount Columbia, next to Mount Yale. An army Chinook helicopter from Fort Carson was brought in to help on the morning of the second day of the search. A Chinook is a giant helicopter with two rotors used to move large cargo, like a flying 18-wheeler. It is powerful enough to fly rescuers in and out at high altitudes.

The Chinook ferried searchers to the Mount Columbia area that morning. Tracks were found in the snow, but they were quickly determined to be unrelated to the crash. Searchers continued to use the Chinook over the next three days to shuttle searchers into and out of the Mount Columbia area to cover as much ground as possible.

Eventually members from mountain rescue teams throughout Colorado arrived in Buena Vista, including teams from Vail, Alpine, Summit County, and El Paso County. A contingent of RMR rescuers arrived at 3 A.M. on the third day of the search. They were equipped with their own DF gear and had the expertise to use it on a ground search. RMR began to question the search area, based on the readings they had taken.

On day four of the search, rescuers still had not found the ELT, and weather conditions were not getting better. It had now been five days since the crash. They had not found any other clues or indications of an airplane wreck. If there was a crash, the chances of survival were believed to be minimal, decreasing with each passing day. The ELT signal was fading noticeably as its battery gave out. The environment was dangerous because of weather and avalanche potential, and each hour increased the chances of searchers getting hurt or killed. The mission leader had already considered scrubbing the mission twice before, and this time it seemed to be the right choice. But there was still that pesky and persistent ELT signal.

The RMR team was becoming more convinced that CAP had been directing the search in the wrong area. They should be looking on Mount Yale. As rumor spread that the mission would be called off, RMR member Bruce Bartram decided to take action. He had a highly visible and heated argument with the mission leaders; he wanted to keep searching for the ELT while they had a signal. He pushed for at least one more day of searching, but this time on Mount Yale. Here was a team willing to keep searching if the mission leaders were willing to continue the mission. The mission leader was swayed and gave Bruce and the RMR team one more day.

At noon of the sixth day since the crash, rescuers were flown to the site that RMR believed was the most likely place to find the wreck. They would have to give up their search at the agreed-upon time of 4 P.M. As the afternoon search wore on, the RMR team received a stronger signal. They broke trail through deep snow until just after 3:30 P.M. when RMR member Ken Zafren spotted wreckage. He quickly ran over to the site and saw movement. Survivors. Survivors! Bruce radioed back to mission base, "We have found wreckage and there are survivors!"

The few people left at mission base were absolutely shocked and elated.

The evacuation of the four family members took another day. All of them recovered after spending six days injured in sub-zero temperatures with little water, no food, and flimsy shelter high in the Colorado Rockies. Much credit goes to the scores of volunteer rescuers who helped with the search and evacuation. But had it not been for the ELT and the persistence and expertise of RMR, the crash victims would not have been found alive in the last hour of the last search day.

Pioneers

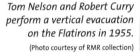

Tom Nelson and Robert Curry
perform a vertical evacuation
on the Flatirons in 1955.
(Photo courtesy of RMR collection)

It was a cold weekend in 1962 when two Boulder teenagers set out to climb a difficult route called Yellow Spur in Eldorado Canyon. Their energy and enthusiasm compelled them to attempt a long climb, and their inexperience got them into trouble. As is typical in Colorado, the weather that day started out reasonable, but deteriorated into a snowstorm by the afternoon as the boys were high on the rock wall. They tried to retreat but became stranded far from the ground. Their parents called RMR when the boys failed to return home in the growing storm.

RMR responded. A climber ascended to the T-shirt-clad teenagers and helped them down. It was 7 P.M. by the time the rescuer reached the boys in the winter storm. The boys were Larry Dalke (age 16) and Pat Ament (age 15). Both went on in later years to make first ascents of extremely difficult rock routes in Boulder and beyond, and achieved fame in the rock-climbing world. Their rescuer was none other than the legendary Layton Kor, Boulder's first world-class climber. Kor knew what he was in for when he volunteered for the rescue; he had been the first person to climb the route a few years earlier.

Kor was not an official member of RMR but remained on the "to-call" list when difficult rescues demanded his amazing climbing skills. Kor's prolific climbing career included a multitude of first ascents in Boulder, wider Colorado, and beyond. He was a member of the team that made the first winter ascent of the giant and dangerous north face of the Eiger in Switzerland.

Kor and partner Ray Northcutt wanted to make the first ascent of the Diamond on Longs Peak during the summer of 1960. They were "Colorado boys" who had seemingly earned the right to claim the first ascent of arguably the most difficult big wall in the United States. The National Park Service forbade climbing on the Diamond, so Kor and Northcutt changed their plans and made the first ascent of a wall just below the Diamond called the Diagonal, proving that successful big-wall climbing at high altitude was possible. Soon after, the Park Service opened up the Diamond for climbing.

Fortune frowned on Kor and Northcutt, who were not in Colorado when the Park Service relented and gave permission to Dave Rearick and Bob Kamps to climb the Diamond. Because the Park Service was concerned about the possibility of a rescue on the difficult face, they imposed a condition on Rearick and Kamps: they had to provide their own rescue team, which would be on standby at the base of the cliff during the climb.

Rearick asked Baker Armstrong (an RMR leader at the time) if RMR would be their rescue team. Armstrong refused, saying they wanted to back the "Colorado boys" Kor and Northcutt. So Rearick asked the Alpine Rescue Team and they agreed. Their climb was a success, and Rearick and Kamps became heroes. *Time* magazine recognized them as America's most daring climbers.

Rearick has lived in Boulder ever since his climb of the Diamond and is a true "Colorado boy" by any measure. I asked Rearick, a retired professor of mathematics at the University of Colorado, if he had any recollections of RMR. He recalled that he helped with a rescue of a badly hurt climber in Eldorado Canyon at some point. He also said that sometime after his Diamond climb, Armstrong asked him if he was interested in being group leader of RMR (apparently now having gained Armstrong's respect). He laughed, recalled Armstrong's refusal to help, and politely declined the invitation.

During the first few decades of RMR's existence, volunteers for rescue ranged from the very talented and driven climbers, such as Kor, to more moderate hiking enthusiasts of the Colorado Mountain Club. "All the serious climbers at that time were also in RMR," admitted Boulder climbing icon Gerry Roach, who began his climbing career while hanging out with the group. Roach went on to become the second person to climb the Seven Summits, the highest points on all the continents. Closer to home, he has been prolific in both climbing, and guidebook production. He is the first person to have climbed the highest fifteen mountains in North America, which include some very difficult Alaskan peaks. His guidebooks run the gamut from rock climbs around Boulder to routes on the Fourteeners. Roach was introduced to the high peaks by RMR at the age of fourteen. He went on many group practices and learned about technical rope rigging. Not only did he gain experience with climbing, he learned firsthand the terrible consequences of accidents in the mountains. "That's one reason I've stayed alive all these years, and I can thank Rocky Mountain Rescue for some of my training," he said in 2006.

Perhaps the most illustrious mountaineer associated with RMR is Tom Hornbein. He is a retired professor emeritus of anesthesiology and physiology and biophysics at the University of Washington in Seattle. He was a student at the University of Colorado from 1948 to 1952, during the founding years of RMR. He became a prolific climber, making first ascents in the Flatirons (the Willy B. and Friday's Folly and the Northwest Passage on the Third Flatiron among them), in Rocky Mountain National Park (Zumie's Thumb is one), and in the Himalayas.

In 1963, he and partner Willi Unsoeld made the first ascent of the west ridge of Mount Everest, an astounding feat. They decided to descend the easier South Col route where they met two other teammates who had summitted hours earlier and were descending. All four ended up having to bivvy overnight above 28,000 feet in the open and without supplemental oxygen. All survived with some frostbite. They descended the next morning, Hornbein and Unsoeld having completed the first traverse of a major Himalayan peak. It was a revolutionary advance in Himalayan climbing and the seventh ascent of Everest, depicted in the book *Everest, the West Ridge*.

Tom is legendary in mountaineering circles. I was surprised when I found out he was group leader of RMR in 1951 and 1952 and had signed the original certificate of incorporation. I contacted Tom hoping to gain some insight to the founding days of Rocky Mountain Rescue.

Long after Tom's tenure in RMR, he settled in the Northwest where he was also somewhat involved in mountain rescue. Mountain rescue began in Colorado and the Northwest, concurrent but independently. Sometimes there are good-natured disputes about "who did things first." The Mountain Rescue Association (MRA) was initially organized in the Northwest in the 1950s. Tom's perception was that events developed independently and in parallel between the Northwest and Colorado.

"The Mountain Rescue Council (which later became the MRA) of Seattle and RMR started about the same time, I guess in 1947 or 1948," said Tom, who was present during the foundation of mountain rescue in Colorado and an early participant in the Northwest. "My memories of when I started there at CU as a freshman student in the fall of 1948, is the organization. [RMR] I guess was just starting. I wasn't one of the creators of it; it was there when I got there. It hadn't been there very long actually, so I was probably among the initial bunch to a certain extent."

He had discovered RMR as a student. "The people who were in it [RMR] were the people also climbing . . . Bill Braddock and Bob Riley were my initial climbing partners . . . The Willy B. was my creation after Bill, and play on words: 'Will He Be.' Sort of the mentality of a young freshman, I suppose."

Tom began his outdoor adventures in Colorado long before college. "I'd been a 'camper' at Cheley camp. My parents sent me to Trails End when I was thirteen. The first year the idea of walking anywhere was totally appalling and they made me go on a backpack to Ypsilon Lake. Since I was a little scrawny runt they put all the Tasty bread in my pack. By the time we got there it was all compressed because I'd lean on trees every time we stopped. I found that going downhill was a lot easier and that took away all the fear, I guess, and the next year I started doing it on my own."

Not only did Tom discover the freedom and enjoyment of hiking, he began exploring the ubiquitous rock outcroppings in the high mountains. "We did a lot of scrambling and things no one should be doing without proper technique. Our counselors were not smart enough to know. Fortunately, no one fell off of anything and got hurt. By the time I was a counselor I was seriously climbing. That would be in my college years.

"My first college student climb was with Bill Braddock. The CMC had just come out with an issue of the *Trail and Timberline* or something with route descriptions for the Flatirons. So we got this 30-foot piece of probably one-inch-diameter rope and headed up to 1911 Gulley [on the Third Flatiron] with the instruction book in one hand and the rope over our shoulders, and climbed up the route. When we got to these slightly overhanging places, one of us would climb over it carrying the rope and uncoil it and drop it down for the other person to hold on to if they needed. We weren't tied into it. We soon learned how to tie bowlines, to tie in and belay using manila ropes, picking the splinters out of our hands for a while."

Today, Boulder is a mecca for rock climbers. Thousands of technical-climbing pilgrims from around the world visit to pay homage to the Boulder rock formations, and thousands of others make their home here. But there were far fewer climbers in Boulder in the early 1950s, and those climbers shared the duty of mountain rescue. It was a natural affinity for Tom as he became an important, though younger, member of the Rescue Group.

"I think the original [RMR] group was Dex Brinker and Bruce Snow, Tom Taylor, and Wes Horner. They were former 10th Mountain Division types who were a few years older than I was."

They practiced brand new techniques. "I remember the first time we ever lowered a litter was sort of my instigation ... We took this litter and a young woman classmate, who was also studying to be a geologist, Marty Slawson, and we stuffed her into this litter. We went up on the face of the Third Flatiron and hooked up through those eyebolts and started lowering like the Germans did in the books we read. When we came down the sheriff was waiting at the Bluebell shelter (you could drive up there in those days). He was very kind but said 'Next time you decide to do this, let us know ahead of time so that when someone sees you they know it's not some big disaster and don't call the sheriff.' That was the first litter lowering. You tied into a rope with a bowline around your waist. Life was simple in those days."

Tom recalled the early initiative of the group in practicing techniques that had never been performed by a mountain rescue team in Colorado. "We just did it. Our bible was Wastl Mariner's book [on mountain rescue], written in German; I don't think it was translated at the time. We studied the drawings. That's where we learned about the carabiner brake, how to put it together, and this was our first attempt to go up and see how it really worked. I think the same things we were doing there were going on concurrently in the Northwest ... The two [rescue groups] started at the same time quite independent of each other."

Tom recalled other innovations of the group during the early days. "We worked a lot on the Stokes litter. We figured out that it was kind of long, hard to carry around in one piece, so we cut it in half and twisted little pipes in the tubing to join it back together. We put it onto army surplus plywood pack frames to carry. We played around with the wheel a little bit, but never got it to work well."

"I remember when we were doing these litter lowerings, the biggest challenge was that the ropes were 120 feet long and the stuff we used to lower off in Boulder Canyon was longer than that, so the challenge was, of course, to be able to connect one rope to another and get the knot past a carabiner brake and do it fairly smoothly [this was our first knot pass technique]. What it involved was using a Prusik [a knot that is used in mountaineering] to anchor the rope while you rebuilt the brake on the uphill side of the knot when you got to the knot. Then you would pop the Prusik; it had a loop that was going to a carabiner with an angle piton. You'd pull the piton out and everything would suddenly drop about a foot or two. The poor guy was the one holding the stretcher out from the wall. It was always very exciting, but it worked . . . Just kind of slow and ponderous."

"Some of the other things that I recall doing were first-aid classes. Also, lots of square dances in Roy and Alice Holubar's basement. Holubar was the source of much of the RMR rescue equipment. In their basement they had all sorts of stuff, European ropes and pitons and all that; Alice used to make some beautiful, beautiful clothes."

Though they formed a strong foundation of rescue skill and innovative technique, the early days of the group saw difficulty in gaining real experience. Tom remembered, "If you get down to what we did in terms of actual rescues, I'd say it was damn little. I can remember tromping around searching for a few lost souls and never finding them. We never did a technical rescue. When people fell off the Flatirons you tended to pick them up at the bottom."

Tom, however, credits Rocky Mountain Rescue with helping to give him a clear direction in life. "I came to Boulder to become a geologist. I got involved in climbing, mountain rescue, then learning and then teaching first aid. At the end of my junior year I decided I didn't want to be a geologist anymore so I applied to medical school. I didn't have all the requirements for pre-med, so in my senior year I had to overlap labs in order to get everything done. One of the labs [chemistry] was taught by Harry Walton [an RMR founder]. He was very understanding and allowed me to work in the lab on my own time. When it came to a grade he said 'I'm sorry, Tom, but since you weren't at the regular lab I had to give you a B instead of an A.' He was really very nurturing of me. So I would say mountain rescue was a tipping point toward my career in medicine." We ended our conversation with the recollection of his climb of Everest with Willi Unsoeld. I said, "You guys were amazingly strong on Everest; you don't see many people doing that today." Tom's typically honest, but humble, response was, "Well I don't know, we didn't know what we were doing, we were just doing what we did in Colorado and just kept climbing ... I should also say that today is the thirty-ninth anniversary of our Everest climb." I interviewed Tom on May 22, 2002, the anniversary of his and Unsoeld's ascent via the Hornbein Couloir in 1963.

Summer

*"When you go up to the mountain too often,
you will eventually encounter the tiger."*

ANCIENT CHINESE PROVERB

Deadman Gulch

Scree evac in progress.
(Photo courtesy of Jeff Sparhawk)

I WAS HOT, TIRED, AND THIRSTY. I wiped alkaline sweat from my forehead with my drenched shirt. I had been tracking up and down steep, tree-covered slopes on a sweltering early summer afternoon looking for signs of a missing hiker. I was one of dozens of searchers combing a labyrinth of hills and cliffs in the foothills of north Boulder County. The radio had been crackling with traffic, teams reporting positions, receiving assignments, and confirming search areas, all the normal logistics of a massive operation.

It was about 6 P.M. when everyone heard a weak, broken signal full of static. It was barely intelligible but very different from the communications of the last hours. I recognized Shelly's voice. She had found John Wade, the missing party, and he was seriously injured. Shelly's signal was faint, as if some mysterious energy-dampening force was trying to block her radio, but the communication from command was loud and frantically clear: "Repeat ... Repeat ... What is your location? Repeat ..." I could decipher the phonemes "De———-Gul—." I knew where she was, Deadman Gulch, a deep ravine east of my location. She was in the bottom of the gulley, which prevented clear radio communication. I began jogging toward the gulch. The search had transformed into a rescue.

The mission began at 2:45 P.M. on May 16. The weather that day was exquisite, and I was lamenting being trapped indoors slaving away in front of a computer screen. This day was a perfect hint of the summer to come during a wet and stormy springtime: hot, windless, and not a thunderstorm in sight.

The page called for RMR to search for an eighty-one-year-old male who was missing from his hiking group. The group had been on a small mountain west of Lyons. The missing person had left the main group, deciding to turn back while the main party went on to the summit. When the group returned to the trailhead, the missing person's car had not moved and they had not seen him on their descent. The summit of the mountain they were climbing is at 8,049 feet, but rises only 1,700 feet from the trailhead, and was only a mile and a half away. The terrain surrounding the summit route was rugged, steep, and strewn with cliffs, but it is considered an easy hike if one stays on the trail.

Most incidents of a reported missing hiker in the middle of a nice day in Boulder County are benign. A concerned family member or friend, alarmed about someone unexpectedly absent from an appointed meeting time, sometimes calls for help even though the circumstances don't necessarily warrant an emergency response. RMR responds. This case would seem to fall into that category except for two disturbing facts: the missing man, John Wade, was a very experienced and responsible hiker and should have been back to his car long before the rest of his party. And though competent, his age was a distressing factor.

I arrived at the command center set up at the trailhead parking lot in South Saint Vrain Canyon and was soon in the field as a one-man search team—I could cover ground more quickly that way. Other RMR search teams were already in the field. They were joined by sheriff's deputies, firefighters, and search dogs. As time went on with no sign of Wade, the level of urgency escalated and soon a helicopter was called to search from the air. The sun was setting, but the weather remained warm. I methodically scrutinized my assigned area, looking around crags, ravines, and trees. I could hear the helicopter droning in the distance. Occasionally it would pass overhead with its loud, mechanical thumping momentarily filling the air. Despite the commanding view and quick coverage possible from the air, they saw no sign of Wade.

I checked the coordinates on my GPS receiver and verified my location on my U.S. Geological Survey quadrangle map. I radioed in my position and status to command. The only clues I had found were tracks from other searchers. In the four hours since Wade was last seen, no one had found a clue as to his whereabouts. Wade's last known position was in a wooded, relatively flat area. There was no trail there and Wade left no track.

I recalled hiking in this area two years prior and noting the flat ground and lack of terrain signs that would allow me to ramble without thinking much about my direction. I had to pay attention to where I was going; the forest hid any navigational landmarks. It would be easy to get off-course here and descend the wrong valley, but a directional mistake would be noticed long before any dangerous terrain was encountered, and it would be easy to avoid such terrain.

At approximately 5:10 P.M. RMR received another page. There was a kayak accident at the south end of Boulder County. We were now challenged with a massive search and an obligation to respond to this new incident. A few members broke off and began the drive to Rollinsville where the accident occurred. Soon after, RMR's response was cancelled. The kayaker was killed and other agencies were able to recover the body. RMR could continue the search-in-progress with full personnel, but there was a foreboding tenseness in the air.

The number of search personnel grew steadily. Shelly was one of the last people to join in the search, having been unable to leave work at the initial page. She and another searcher were assigned an area in a rugged ravine called Deadman Gulch, well outside the areas of high probability of a find.

They climbed up the steep, shrub- and poison ivy–choked ravine, thinking that no one in his right mind would be in such a place. They called out "John" regularly as they searched, hardly expecting a response. Near the top of the gulch, the walls turn to difficult-to-climb moss-covered cliff faces. As Shelly called out "John!" her search partner heard a muffled moan coming from a brush-covered cove to their left. They climbed over a difficult rock face and found Wade. He was semiconscious with massive trauma to his head and thorax. He was alive but in terrible condition. Shelly called out the situation on her rescue radio. No one could hear her clearly, as if the force that pulled Wade into the ground was also trying to kill Shelly's radio signal.

All the search teams spread out over several square miles of the search area immediately began hiking toward the accident site. The teams near the command center went there to carry the evac equipment into the field. Rescuers were soon humping heavy rescue loads up the gulch, fighting the shrubs and hedges as they carried 60 pounds on their backs. They carried the litter, bean bag, ropes, bash kit, and advanced first-aid kit, as well as their personal gear.

Meanwhile Shelly and her partner, a Boulder County Open Space ranger, could do little for John except wait for an evac. Shelly put her jacket over John to keep him warm in the fading daylight. The ranger, who was at first relieved that John had been found, was now becoming distraught as the reality of the situation sunk in. The ranger assumed the search helicopter he heard would be used to extract John. "I told him I didn't think it was possible," Shelly said later. She was right. The terrain was far too jagged to use a helicopter, and it was not equipped for a hovering loading. There was no landing zone within a mile.

I approached the gulch from the upper end where I had to descend treacherously loose and vegetated slopes. Progress from any direction was extremely difficult. Night was descending upon us. I arrived at the accident site as the last minutes of daylight faded.

As we arrived at the victim from all points on the compass, we could now see Wade was lying on a ledge on the side of the ravine. Paramedics immediately began advanced life support. A technical evacuation was necessary and would not be ready before it was pitch dark. Of greater concern was how to carry the victim out through the dense bushes and thickets below. The Lyons Fire Department volunteers had an idea: They began brute-force cutting of a trail through the underbrush using chain and hand saws. Soon the patient was packaged in the litter and on his way down. The paramedics were close-by "bagging" the victim, a procedure that forced air into his lungs with an air bladder. We were on our way in a desperate attempt to save Wade.

How Wade ended up in such a predicament is truly a mystery. The terrain in the area was generally safe and easy, except for the occasional large and avoidable cliff. Wade was found in probably the most technically difficult descent down the mountain. What had happened? If you were to plot John's last-seen position and direction of travel on a map, it points in the general direction of his car at the parking lot. It also points roughly to where he was found. Apparently, he had started his descent in the right direction but got confused in the woods and made a slight deviation northward. With no landmarks or trail to point the way, he compounded his error with each step. But by no means was this a fatal error, merely an inconvenience at most when he finally ended up at the road, a mile from his car.

He walked down what began as a mildly sloping ravine. It steepened almost imperceptibly at first. As the slope descends, it eventually becomes alarmingly precipitous. The vegetation at the bottom of the ravine, the shallowest sloping part, is covered with thick brush and trees that make it impossible to navigate. The only passable way is to scramble sidehill down the walls of the gully, which are also covered with loose rock and vegetation. Wade had done this and was just above what he probably thought was the last difficult move when he fell. He probably lost his footing on a steep wall and fell maybe twenty feet to the ledge where he was found, hidden among the copious bushes near the bottom of the ravine, impossible to see from the air.

We'll never know why Wade hadn't turned around when the slope started getting dangerous. A possible explanation is that he simply thought he could climb out of the situation even as it was getting difficult. He was possibly tired or not feeling well (thus the reason for leaving his group in the first place) and felt that going down a short difficult section was easier than retracing his route uphill for another half hour. Many avid hikers have made the same decision in similar situations. It's possible that, motivated by the desire to get down quickly, his judgment was clouded a bit and he climbed into a bad situation.

It was now dark, but still warm and muggy in the ravine. The firefighters had finished their hard labor of cutting a path, greatly easing the evac difficulty but not eliminating it. I had been alternating belaying and carrying the litter. The litter bearers were sweating profusely as the paramedics closely monitored John's condition at each step. John had been intubated, a procedure performed to control John's breathing. He had given up on the ultimate drive of life. We continued to carry John and the litter, more than 200 awkward pounds, through the brush, rocks, and standing water in the ravine.

Sometime during the carry down, near midnight, John died of his massive injuries. Rescuers continued with their job, but the urgency ended. There was one last belay point above the mouth of the ravine. Brakes were set up and the familiar "Down Slow" command was given. The ravine opened up and met Highway 7. The rescue team arrived with their patient at midnight. John's body was loaded in the back of an ambulance, and it drove away slowly, emergency lights off.

Shelly and I walked to my car. I took off my pack and boots and sat down. As I decompressed from the rescue, I noticed the large number of people now milling around at the trailhead. There were more than sixty people helping with this search/rescue/evac. Everyone was tired and somewhat somber. The Salvation Army brought us sandwiches and drinks, which gave a little relief from the letdown. Exhausted and emotionally drained, Shelly and I drove the short distance home in the early morning darkness.

Wade was an eminently experienced mountaineer, having led outings for the Sierra Club for decades. He died doing what he loved, but his fate left a haunting legacy. The incredulous accident that killed him around midnight was in Deadman Gulch, on the slopes of a mountain called Coffintop.

Outrageous Fortune

Steep scree evacuation.
(Photo courtesy of Jeff Sparhawk)

ON ANY GIVEN WEEKEND DAY during summer in Boulder, there are hundreds of technical rock climbers ascending their choice of a myriad of routes strung along the crags and rock faces lying along a line running from Eldorado Canyon to Boulder Canyon. One hot Sunday afternoon in August 1999 witnessed two of these climbers getting a leisurely start, hitting the Royal Arch trail above Chautauqua Park after noon. Their goal was an exceptionally remote route located high on Green Mountain above the Fourth Flatiron.

Both of these climbers were experts, possessing both the physical ability necessary to scale difficult rock faces and advanced knowledge of climbing methodology to do it safely. The heat from the noontime sun of high summer was their main concern as they ascended the steep trail below Sentinel Pass. The pass is a high point along the trail to the Royal Arch, a popular hiking destination to a natural stone archway. Hikers on their way to the arch are rewarded by a downhill section of trail beyond the pass. The route to the climbing partners' destination, however, deviated off the Royal Arch trail at this pass. They bushwhacked through pine deadfall and over boulders for several hundred more feet of elevation gain, where they finally arrived at their goal. They stopped, rested in the sweltering sun, organized their climbing rope and rock placement gear, put on their harnesses, and began their ascent.

At the same time, six miles to the northwest in Dream Canyon, a steep gorge just above the popular tourist spot of Boulder Falls in Boulder Canyon, RMR was on a training exercise practicing long cable evacuations. We were training with the backpackable power cable winch, a gas-powered engine that could raise or lower the litter and its attendants quickly and efficiently, for evacuations up or down very long distances.

I was one of four litter bearers, now standing at the bottom of Dream Canyon, having just been lowered down 1,000 feet over steep rock faces and dirt slopes. We were resting before the ascent back up to the rim. We had just set the litter on the ground. My fingers were stiffened into a gripping position from holding the litter off the ground. I pressed my fingers against my leg, bending them back straight and pulled off my grime-stained gloves with my teeth. The leather was permeated with sweat. I wiped my face, the bandana tied around my head beneath my helmet was saturated and could not absorb any more water. We savored a few minutes of rest before regrouping. Soon the litter captain called "Up Slow!" on his packset, and we began the slow, straining ascent up the face.

After what seemed like an eternity of epic struggle over cliffs and clefts, sand and gravel, logs and underbrush, the world looked cloudy through my sunglasses. The edges were blurred by the residue of dried sweat, the center wavy from fresh sweat dripping down from my brow. But we were finally at the top, finished. At this time I was a new member, so I had won the "prize" of being a litter bearer for an entire up-and-down evac cycle. I toughed it out, but was now dehydrated and hungry, looking forward to being immediately satiated with a few quarts of water and then a late meal after practice.

Jim Gallo, also a new member, and I drove down Boulder Canyon, intending to devour a meal at the Dark Horse, a local watering hole in Boulder. As we drove into the parking lot anticipating a meal that would fill us up for days or possibly a week, our pagers sparked to life with a call for a rescue: "RMR respond to a climbing accident at Green Mountain Butte." What? We'd never heard of the place. But the excitement of a rescue overwhelmed both our hunger and confusion about the location, and we mentally prepared for a rescue. The next information we heard on the radio clarified the location. It was Green Mountain Pinnacle, a rock outcropping above the Fourth Flatiron.

We drove west on Baseline Road, up to Chautauqua Park. There is an access road from Chautauqua to Bluebell shelter. The gate to this road is normally closed but was now open to give us quick access. We drove up the bumpy road to the shelter, as curious and confused hikers and joggers stepped aside.

1970 was already there, its large double doors swung wide open in back, having driven hot from downtown Boulder up through "The Hill" area in west Boulder. Jim parked his truck; we hopped out and grabbed our packs. Though I wasn't able to grab even a small snack, I did rehydrate and was ready to go, invigorated by the adrenaline of the rescue.

We went to the back of 1970 where Jim shouldered two 200-foot ropes. I grabbed one rope and the bash kit, adding 40 pounds to the weight already in my pack. Glen Delman put the 45-pound litter on his back. An ultra-marathoner, Glen viewed this job as an opportunity to train for a marathon, and to our collective amazement began running up the steep trail with the huge load in the 95-degree heat. Feeling somewhat less energetic, I set a rapid hiking pace and watched him disappear in the trees ahead of me.

Equipment was sent into the field in groups as people arrived. The most critical equipment is sent first: for most rescues, first-aid kits and a jet pack (oxygen bottles) go first. Then comes the litter and bean bag, followed by ropes and anchor equipment. The equipment goes into the field in groups as rescue personnel arrive and check in at 1970. It is soon spread out between the trailhead and the rescue site in a caravan of muscle-powered transport.

This is a difficult part of any rescue. The equipment bearers are slower than the initial responders who get into the field fast to assess the situation, determine the best access, and provide initial medical care. Except for the mission leaders at the trailhead, everyone carries equipment. The information about the route to the accident can be good, scant, or nonexistent if the victim has not been found. But even with the best possible description, the access route to a victim is usually an unknown factor. The equipment bearers begin their journey with a sense of urgency and exhilaration, but must contend with the distance, elevation gain, and environmental conditions.

It's difficult to pace yourself—the starting gun for this race fires at random and the course distance and difficulty are usually a mystery. As each bearer powers his way up the mountain, the finish line is unknown until it's over. Laden with awkward, lumbering loads, the bearers must climb over difficult terrain. Bearers are grateful if the route only involves hiking a steep trail. Most rescue locations require bushwhacking and rock scrambling to access.

Green Mountain Pinnacle was a textbook example of a difficult location. Only about a mile from the trailhead, it requires 1,600 feet of elevation gain, half of which is in steep, densely forested underbrush. A fast hiker with a light pack can cover the distance in 45 minutes.

Jim and I were in the middle of the pack. We hiked at a fast, difficult pace until we reached Sentinel Pass. Here we left the trail and struggled up through the boulders and trees until we finally arrived at the accident site. I was again thirsty, covered in sweat, and tired. Unfortunately, we had plenty of work left to do and so I couldn't let myself rest yet.

I looked around and saw a man lying on his back at the foot of an overhanging rock face, his climbing rope dangling limp above him. Paramedics were already treating him, they had an intravenous tube in his arm and had a cervical spine collar around his neck to help prevent head motion in case he had broken his neck.

I downed a quart of water as I surveyed the rescue scene. The litter was being assembled and ropes tied. I set up a belay anchor on a tree, contemplating how difficult this evacuation would be down the complex terrain below us. I started to hear the story of what happened.

Bill Wright, a well-known local Boulder climber, was the man lying on the ground. Bill and his partner were on a route ironically called Death and Transfiguration, a very difficult technical rock climb up an overhanging cliff. Bill had topped out and started belaying his partner up. His partner repeatedly fell on the lower route and decided to quit and be lowered down to the ground on the rope. Since Bill's partner could not retrieve all of the climbing protective equipment that Bill used as he led up, a job the second on a rope team usually performs, Bill would retrieve his gear by a different method.

Bill anchored the top end of his rope and ran it through his rappel device. He would rappel down and pull each piece as he descended to it. Then he'd climb up the easy back side of the crag and get the rope. He started his rappel and descended to his first piece. He pulled it out and clipped it to his harness. He continued down to the next piece. He pulled it out. It was going smoothly. He approached the overhang. Bill asked his partner on the ground to put him on a "fireman's belay." His partner pulled tension on the rope, taking control of Bill's descent. A fireman's belay is a very effective means of controlling a rappeller from the ground. This allowed Bill to free up his "brake hand," the hand he used to control his rappel, and use both hands to free the next piece while his partner held him in place from the ground.

Bill's partner lowered him a few more feet when both men felt a violent tug on the rope. Bill was in a free fall. What?! He reacted immediately, instinctively grabbing the rope above him as a drowning man desperately flails for anything around him to keep his head above water. Bill's forearms instantaneously flexed, which caused his hand to curl tightly around his lifeline.

A minute amount of kinetic energy building in his free fall was transformed into friction heat and the mechanical tearing of flesh from his hands. A small amount of the energy that melted his skin registered in his consciousness as searing pain but not before his reflexes forced his hand to let go of the rope. His body continued to accelerate toward the rocks below. Perhaps he tried in vain to grab the rope again, perhaps he didn't have time before his body slammed into the unyielding earth, cracking one of his lumbar vertebrae.

Bill's partner was in surprise and shock. Though Bill was alive and miraculously without a head or neck injury, Bill's partner had to get help. Neither had any clue as to how Bill could be saved. His partner descended all the way down to the Royal Arch trail and had someone call for help on a cell phone.

RMR was here now and we had a job to complete. There were 40 of us in the field now and we would get Bill down the mountain. I had recovered and recharged while performing the physically undemanding anchor construction. Everyone was ready for the evac. I didn't think about how long it would take. We always perform one task at a time, and the concentration we put into the job at the moment causes us to lose perception of time as it literally flies by.

Everything was ready, and we were ready to package Bill in the litter. Six rescuers surrounded Bill and carefully lifted him about two feet off the ground, keeping his head and neck immobilized. The litter was slid under him and he was lowered into it. The bean bag was formed around him and the air was evacuated by a hand pump, causing the bag to stiffen and hold his entire body immobile. Bill was then strapped into the litter with four heavy-duty belts along the length of the litter. An oxygen bottle was placed between his legs and the IV bag and blood pressure gauge next to him. A special helmet was put over his head, now taped in place to the bean bag. He was ready to go.

For the evac we would negotiate the mountainside covered with small cliffs and huge logs of downed timber covered in underbrush. The steel litter protecting Bill would be his armored cocoon over this hostile land. One end of a rope was tied onto the litter. I threaded the other end through the brakeplate and signaled the six litter bearers that they were now ready for a safe, controlled descent by calling "On Belay, Stop!"

The litter captain initiated the scree evac by calling "Down Slow!" I let the rope run through the belay device slowly. A scree evac is a mass lowering of people on a rope system. Litter bearers pull back on the litter as they go downhill with their bodies perpendicular to the slope. They are lowered by a belayer on the top end of the rope. This is the safest way to evacuate someone down a rugged, sloping mountain. The victim in the litter is in a much safer position than the bearers themselves. The bearers must fight the terrain, crawling over rocks, tripping over logs, and getting scraped by tree branches. The evac of Bill was particularly nasty.

The litter bearers muscled their burden down the first steep rock face covered with moss and lichen. Six bearers were crowded around the litter, three on each side. Their bodies faced uphill as they gripped the litter railing with one or two hands. Each left-right paired position had its unique difficulties and responsibilities.

The top two, highest on the slope, holding the head end (the victim is normally positioned so that his head is uphill), have less weight to bear than their other comrades so they are saddled with the extra duties of litter captains, who control the descent via radio, and patient monitoring and care, much of which happens at the head end. They must monitor problems with oxygen masks, intubation breathing apparatus (for assisted breathing), and general facial appearance and cognitive ability. They watch for rock or debris falling from above. If a rock happens to tumble down, they bend over and shield the immobilized and vulnerable victim with their own bodies. And they must reassure victims as they descend; a litter ride even with no injury can be quite startling.

The two bearers at the foot, the lowest end, are first down the slope. Like their teammates at the head, they carry less weight and so have another responsibility. They must be the eyes of the other bearers. They watch the route and signal when obstacles approach that require significant maneuvering. It is very difficult for the other bearers to see the ground beneath their feet. They shout "Rock on the left!" or "Hole on the right!" Minor unevenness, the size of which would easily trip an unwary hiker, is expected and no alert is issued. The center two bearers are encumbered with the most physically demanding job. They carry the heaviest portion of weight. They are boxed in by the upper and lower bearers and scarcely have room to walk without bumping into either their upper or lower teammate. They cannot see up or down and must rely on the feel of the ground as they descend. They must do this while holding onto a hefty load. Imagine standing on a steep, grungy slope, facing uphill as you are blindfolded, and then walking backward down the slope while holding a 40-pound barbell to one side, and it is imperative that you never drop the barbell. This is not a medieval torture technique, this is a rescue.

The bearers descended with Bill packaged in tightly, safe in his protective steel casing. The first pitch is steep, the bearers work hard to keep upright on the rock. It is awkward. Feet slip, trip, and recover. The litter is pulled to one side and then another. The bearers suffer numerous minor injuries: shin whacked against a log, arm pinched between the litter and a tree, finger crushed between litter and rock, buttocks bruised by a branch, arm abraised by stone. Muscles are pulled while heaving the litter sideways. The sounds you hear are of tree and bush limbs snapping and the panting and grunting of the bearers as they fight their way down the slope.

Clothing is shredded on snags. Poison ivy rubs on skin, while sweat soaks your clothing and all exposed equipment. After the steep rock face, the bearers must negotiate a gigantic boulder. They stop and set the litter down while the first two bearers climb over the boulder. The litter is handed through while the next two climb over the boulder. This process is repeated until they are back on a steep slope. Soon the belay rope comes to an end, and I radio "Stop at the brakes, end of the rope!" They set the litter down so the paramedics can check blood pressure, breathing, and the IV flow.

They were now 200 feet down. One pitch finished, only ten more to go.

The litter bearers swap out and are replaced often so that the process can continue quickly and smoothly. After the first pitch, I leapfrog my belay system three pitches down the trail and am ready to belay again when the litter reaches my position. Several pitches later I swap my belay equipment for litter-bearing duties and take my turn on the litter until we are finally down to Sentinel Pass.

From the pass we move more quickly and easily. A wheel is attached to the litter and we move at a rapid pace toward the trailhead. Belays are still required, sometime using anchors, and when the trail is not so steep, just a "walking belay" when several rescuers hold the rope in hand as they walk, helping hold the litter back as they walk.

By the time we reached the Royal Arch trail, Bill was fading alarmingly. His skin was turning gray and he was losing his cognitive abilities. He was exhausted due to his injuries. We hurried down the trail to the ambulance waiting at Bluebell shelter. Bill was loaded and taken to the hospital. His prognosis hung ominously in the air.

Back at 1970, the tension of the rescue faded, the relief and relaxation was palpable. The sky was dark and cool. We coiled ropes, repacked the litter and bean bag, and accounted for all carabiners, slings, and radios in the artificial illumination of 1970's work lights. We were done, four hours after the initial page. I suddenly noticed I was deeply hungry. I didn't anticipate that the hectic pace of the day, from the long practice to the difficult mission, would leave me time only for breakfast that morning. My mission now was an uninterrupted transportation of a burger and fries from the Dark Horse kitchen to my stomach.

BILL'S ACCIDENT WAS LATER ANALYZED. His rope was intact, still anchored at the top of the rock. The rope ran through Bill's rappel device as he was lying broken on the ground, and Bill's climbing partner never let go of his fireman's belay. Bill's equipment retrieval technique, devised by someone with years of experience, seemed sound and in fact was used by Bill in the past to retrieve gear. Yet Bill nearly paid with his life for a flaw somewhere.

His equipment was in perfect working order and no anchor failed. This leaves the possibility that either the belayer "failed" or the technique is bad. The belayer had a simple job, was not distracted, and understood the seriousness of the situation. It is highly unlikely anything went wrong with the belay. What remains is the technique. The key event was the violent tug they felt before the fall.

There is an insidiously dangerous flaw in what Bill was attempting, and these two experts missed it. It wasn't out of carelessness or inexperience, but of a misunderstanding of the nonobvious physics. The fireman's belay only works if the rope can be held in tension at all times. The problem with Bill's situation was the overhang. The rope ran up the face and curved outward around the overhang. As Bill rappelled under the control of the fireman's belay, the tension on the rope was affected by the force applied to it by the rock protection he was trying to remove. If that tension was lost because the piece was removed or pulled out on its own, the rappel brake would be lost and Bill would fall free. Had the rope been free hanging, there would have been no way to lose tension in this manner.

Each protection piece was placed in such a way as to protect the ascending climber from a vertical fall above the point of protection. Rock protection usually does not hold when pulled in a direction other than that which it was placed to hold, in this case a downward fall. A force that pulled the piece horizontally would likely detach the protection from the rock.

As Bill descended on the rope tensioned by his partner below, the rope itself pulled a protection piece horizontally away from the wall, causing tension to be lost. This was the cause of the tug they both felt before Bill's free fall. It wasn't actually a tug but an immediate slackening of the rope.

The system they used to retrieve gear was not standard. Bill was not tied into the rope as is the usual case for this type of gear retrieval when a belayer on the ground is lowering a partner. Also, Bill could have controlled his own rappel, tying himself off if he needed to use two hands. They could not have used the first technique since their rope was not long enough, and the second technique takes longer and is more difficult than the fireman's belay technique.

When the rock protection pulled out, the tension on the rope, which was controlling Bill's descent, was lost. The partner on the ground had no way of regaining this tension in time to stop Bill's crashing descent and Bill hit the ground. His descent was slowed somewhat by his own instinctive but ultimately futile effort to grab the rope. This quite possibly saved his life.

Mistakes are made by everyone. Mountain accident victims are not limited to the ignorant or overconfident newbies. They sometimes catch the best climbers despite their best efforts. With luck they survive with a hard lesson learned.

Bill is an incredible athlete who made an almost miraculous

recovery from his broken back. He still climbs and his specialty is to speed climb technical routes.

There was a happy ending to this mission. But the inescapable conclusion is that Bill was lucky. His accident may have been bad fortune, but his survival was fantastically good luck. There is no argument that Bill is an accomplished climber who over the years has had many successes while gaining countless hours of climbing experience. His mistake was to use a technique in a situation that he hadn't tested before, and which proved to have a critical flaw. RMR picks up the bodies of accomplished but all too human climbers on a regular basis. One of the classic mistakes they make is to try something different, seemingly correct but with a critical flaw that exposes them to death and transfiguration.

Vision on
Apache Peak

*Victim being evacuated by air
ambulance. Queen's Way
couloir in the background.*
(Photo courtesy of Mark Scott-Nash)

THE SUMMIT OF APACHE PEAK IS ISOLATED. It lies at 13,441 feet above sea level on the Continental Divide, near the geographic center of the Indian Peaks wilderness area west of Boulder, 4.5 miles from the nearest trailhead at Brainard Lake. For climbers, it has a long approach and technical routes, all far from the trappings, comforts, and safety of civilization.

At the base of Apache Peak is a large snowfield called Isabelle Glacier. Queen's Way, a name coined by Gerry Roach in his climbing guide to the area, is a narrow finger of snow that extends up from Isabelle Glacier. It is a steep, narrow couloir inset into cliff bands, the top ending on the upper slopes of Apache Peak. Both climbers and backcountry skiers use this permanent snow route. Late in the summer the snow consolidates into a hard, icy mass that increases the climbing difficulty.

On the morning of July 25, 2004, a pair of mountaineers left the Brainard Lake trailhead intent on climbing Apache Peak via the Queen's Way couloir. They walked on the trail past Long Lake and Isabelle Lake. They hiked past a large waterfall above timberline as they ascended to a shelf covered by Isabelle Glacier and a round, deep blue tarn (a small, steep-banked mountain lake or pool). When they arrived at Isabelle Glacier, they removed their ice axes from their packs and began to ascend the sun-hardened snow. The slope steepened to 35 degrees as they entered the narrow couloir.

They gained altitude rapidly and the dizzying exposure increased.

The woman was growing weary having to kick steps and jam her ice axe in the consolidated snow, knowing one misstep would be disastrous. After several hundred feet, her fatigue and anxiety convinced her to give up. She did not feel she could complete the climb safely, and they had no rope. Their best option was to retreat. They began to downclimb.

It was 2:19 P.M. on a Sunday afternoon. I had been cutting branches from overgrown trees in my yard, a mundane chore in the heat of the day. I had been working for several hours, making good progress when my pager squawked to life: "Rocky Mountain Rescue, respond to a fallen climber on Queen's Way." I knew Queen's Way, having climbed it several times. The first thought that entered my mind: this would be a long mission.

I dropped my yard accouterments, jumped into my car, and steered it toward Brainard Lake, about 45 minutes away. I turned on my rescue radio and heard a request for "Helicopter 185" to fly a rapid-response team up to the victim. A good idea, since Queen's Way was a long distance in from the trailhead.

Most RMR rescuers had responded much faster than I and were already well up into the mountains. I happened to be fairly close to the airport and knew the area around Apache Peak well. I radioed Jon Horne, who was coordinating the mission from Boulder, and volunteered to ride up in the first team. He ordered me to respond to the airport along with Clint Dillard, an RMR member and paramedic who could provide advanced life support if necessary.

"Helicopter 185" is the radio designation for an Aerospatiale 315B Lama helicopter contracted by Boulder County that summer to help fight wildfires. RMR makes use of helicopters on rare occasions when the weather, location, and state of the victim make it practical. Helicopter rescues are not the norm and are statistically dangerous in search and rescue work. The thin air at high altitude, as well as the gusty, swirling winds normally present in the mountains, make it a hostile environment for a chopper.

This is about as close as RMR gets to resembling the Rocky Mountain Rescue portrayed in the film *Cliffhanger*. Though the movie inspired at least one member to join RMR, it was not an accurate portrayal of any mountain rescue team. The subject of the film is a mountain rescue team named "Rocky Mountain Rescue" based in Rocky Mountain National Park. There are four likeable and incredulously gullible rescuers who hang out in their cool alpine cabin-style headquarters with their own helicopter parked outside. They sip steaming mugs of hot chocolate and doodle in abstract painting while waiting for rescue calls on their radio base station.

Hollywood's romanticized version aside, RMR has around sixty members, no helicopter, and no permanent headquarters. The group is made up of mostly ordinary people who have real jobs such as lawyers, computer programmers, accountants, engineers, and teachers. The artists in RMR prefer to work in their studios, not at the RMR office that occupies the corner of a meeting room, space donated by Pridemark Paramedic Services.

The weather was fantastic, so there was a high probability a chopper response would work. Clint and I arrived at the Boulder County airport and donned flight suits. We understood the dangers and risks associated with a chopper flight to the high country. Terry Olson was there with litter, bean bag, first-aid kit, ropes, and jet pack. All of the equipment is weighed and packed on the helicopter skid cargo cages. Clint and I buckled into the back seats and strapped on our heavy crash helmets. The pilot sat front left and asked for a radio check. I pushed the helmet-mounted noise-cancelling microphone to my mouth and said, "Radio check." I heard his response through my headphones, "Loud and clear." The turbines started to whine, and the main rotor slowly spun up over our heads. Within minutes we were lifted dead vertically from the tarmac as if in a glass elevator.

Helicopter 185 has more window area than most choppers, allowing nearly 360 degrees of visibility. Suddenly we had a seemingly omniscient vision of the surrounding landscape. The city of Boulder fell below us as we rose, laid out in a chaotic grid on the flat land below. After rising a thousand feet we turned west. Before and below us I saw the abruptly rising foothills, a natural barrier that appeared to be a dam holding back the flood of urbanization to the east. I saw a wide panorama from the Flatirons south to Carter Lake near Loveland in the north. We flew directly over the summit of Mount Sanitas, where I saw hikers streaming like ants up the east ridge trail.

As we flew over the initial wall of mountains, I was struck by the vastness of the textured forests lying between Boulder and the high peaks. I know the area, having driven, biked, and hiked through the area countless times. I studied the land as laid out on topographical and trail maps, and even aerial photos, but viewing this mountainous mural as I glided just a few hundred feet above it, where everything flowed around me in a three-dimensional panorama of trees, hillsides, valleys, and mountaintops, literally added a new perspective to my understanding of the geography. You could explore these mountains your entire life and never go to the same place twice.

We were flying directly west. I saw the town of Ward to our right. Tiny cars moved on the road snaking east down Lefthand Canyon from the town. The forest condensed west of Ward to a thick green carpet, and soon we flew over Brainard Lake, its parking lots brimming with the normal heavy summer traffic. The pilot knew how to get us to Brainard Lake and now he relied on my knowledge to direct him to Apache Peak.

I looked forward out the window and saw a wall of peaks several miles ahead. The top of the wall held towering summits rising higher than our flight level. The conic summits were like paladin guards walking the wall of the Continental Divide. They were bereft of vegetation but covered in a beautiful patchwork of white snow patterns. Small ridges and gulleys lined the gray rock faces.

I was confused. I had never seen these mountains before, yet they were located exactly where Navajo and Apache Peaks should be. I scrambled to find a landmark I could recognize from this viewing angle while the pilot awaited direction. I finally recognized something, the Navajo snowfield. It was wildly distorted from this viewpoint but undeniably correct. It was amazing the difference in the view and the scale of the peaks when looking at them from their height. They appeared much larger, steeper, and intimidating than I had ever witnessed. From the snowfield, I could pick out Navajo Peak, Dickers Peck (yes, this is a real name used to describe a pinnacle north of Navajo Peak), Apache Peak, Isabelle Glacier, and finally Queen's Way. I directed the pilot up the valley.

The pilot flew toward the base of a finger of snow running southwest up Apache Peak. I spotted them at the base of the snow; someone was waving a coat in the air. They were exactly where they said they'd be, always a pleasant, and unusual, surprise in the world of mountain rescue. I pointed them out to the pilot. He circled so close I could see their faces. We now began to look for a landing zone, or LZ.

Less than an hour before, the pair of mountaineers had decided to retreat off the climb, which had quickly proven to be beyond the abilities of the less experienced woman. They began to downclimb.

Though theoretically no more difficult than climbing up, it is generally awkward for inexperienced climbers. Climbing backwards while continuously turning to look down the slope can easily induce vertigo, and she was already in a state of anxiety and tiredness that was building to a dangerous level. She slipped.

She tried to self-arrest in the hard snow but lost control. Self-arresting is a technique used by snow climbers to stop or control a slide down a slope. To self-arrest after a fall, the climber struggles to a head-up-face-down position and, while holding the ice axe close to the torso, digs the pick of the ice axe into the snow, which should act to stop the slide. Hard snow makes this technique difficult to impossible because the pick will skip over the surface, and when it catches the snow may not give, ripping the ice axe out of the grip of the climber. If that happens and the ice axe is not securely attached to the climber, she will lose the axe and have no way to slow her slide.

The woman lost control of her axe and tumbled uncontrollably down the slope. She thudded painfully into the large boulders at the edge of the snow and stopped. After recovering from the sudden shock of falling and crashing, she attempted to stand and walk. She wobbled only a few steps over the boulders before collapsing in pain and weakness. Her partner rapidly descended to her. He had some first-aid training and, after a quick exam, realized she was in trouble. He had packed a cell phone. Luckily, he could reach a cell tower and initiated help immediately. Another pair of hikers in the area came to help.

We scanned in ever-widening circles searching for an LZ. Several times we hovered a few feet above a potential site, only to find a bowling ball–sized rock in the way of a skid. The snowfields were flat but of unknown stability, a skid could punch through and lean the helicopter to one side, the rotor threatening to strike ground. We finally found a spot at the base of the Navajo snowfield. It was about a quarter mile from the victim, not too far to hike.

We landed on a grassy platform at 12,000 feet. The pilot kept the main rotor spinning as we unloaded gear in the loud, windy rotor backwash and cached it 50 feet from the chopper. The pilot and crewman then lifted off as Clint and I sorted gear. I picked up 35 pounds of ropes and anchor gear. Clint grabbed the medical kit and we started a brisk hike toward the victim up a giant rock-covered slope.

Within minutes, we were panting heavily, forcefully inhaling voluminous gulps of air as our circulatory systems labored to deliver sparsely available oxygen to our muscles. I was doing somewhat better than Clint, but ascending 7,000 feet from Boulder in the span of a few minutes is stressful on the respiratory system. Our bodies were not allowed the time to properly adapt to the lower air pressure at this elevation. Nevertheless, we had a job to do and though our lack of acclimatization slowed us and caused more suffering, we were able to continue up the steep slope. I arrived at the scene 20 minutes later, sweating and panting uncontrollably.

As I approached from below, I could see three people standing close together. The victim was lying somewhat comfortably on a flat rock. As soon as my lungs slowed their heaving to a moderate pace, I asked in a broken sentence what had happened. The victim appeared coherent and comfortable as she calmly described her tumble. She had fractured a vertebrae, broken her pelvis, and cracked ribs, but was in surprisingly little pain.

Clint arrived within minutes, sat down, and waited for his breathing to moderate. Several minutes later after his body paid its oxygen debt, he was able to move over and examine her. He confirmed her injuries and felt a helicopter ride out was the best option. It would be much quicker than a litter carry over this high-altitude technical topography.

I radioed the status to the RMR mission base, located at the Long Lake trailhead, who made the decision to call for yet another helicopter, an air ambulance with built-in medical equipment and a flight nurse who could properly care for a seriously injured patient. In the meantime, Helicopter 185 was continuing its job of moving rescuers and gear up the valley, picking them up from mission base and dropping them off at the equipment cache. Another team lead by Jim Gallo had hiked up from the trailhead with a second set of rescue equipment as a backup in case a helicopter evac was impossible for any reason, such as deteriorating weather, oncoming darkness, or mechanical failure.

The next rescuers choppered to the cache site were Chuck Demarest and Lisa Sparhawk. They picked up heavy loads from the gear cache and began the hike up to the victim. Chuck picked up the litter and a rope, about 60 pounds of extra gear, and Lisa shouldered the bean bag and rope, about 45 pounds more than her personal pack. Rich Farnham was next to arrive, but he had traversed a different route. He had jogged the entire distance from the trailhead up the valley to the accident site, and arrived before most of the helicopter-assisted rescuers. Rich, also a paramedic, helped Clint provide expert medical care for the victim. I found myself coordinating a rapidly increasing flurry of activity. Helicopter 185 had found an LZ much closer to the victim, so we now had two equipment caches. Team members were arriving from different directions via two modes, hiking and helicopter. I was making logistical decisions about which gear should move at what time from two different caches. I periodically reported victim medical status, local weather, and general rescue situation to mission base. I made personnel allocation decisions and planned an evacuation route, coordinating the site operations. I gave route directions to approaching rescuers.

Then, at the height of rescue commotion, Jim Gallo radioed we had a second victim.

Jim's team came across a father carrying his son over his shoulder, headed down the trail. They were about a mile down the valley from my location. The son had a broken leg and the father had already carried him several miles. Tired from his long endeavor, he was still a long way from the trailhead over moderately difficult ground. They had serendipitously come across a fully equipped team able to evacuate his son just when he needed it. But we now had simultaneous missions in the same valley.

The radio traffic increased exponentially. On most missions there is an operational channel used to coordinate traffic between the field and command. Mission coordinators use a separate channel to arrange external logistics, such as bringing more rescue supplies to the trailhead or talking with a rescue helicopter. When an evac takes place, a channel is used exclusively for the evacuation traffic. When a litter being lowered needs to call for a "Stop!" it usually needs to stop immediately. With other traffic active on an evac channel, this "Stop!" may not be heard, resulting in a potentially dangerous situation.

This was the norm for a single mission, but now we had two running simultaneously.

We quickly coordinated radio channels. My mission was using radio channel MRA-2, while Jim switched his mission to MRA-1. We used RED-3 for indirectly related mission coordination traffic. We also now had two helicopters operating in the valley. We needed air traffic control. Mission base did most of this coordination, freeing Jim and me to concentrate on fieldwork of our respective missions. My team, though having the more seriously injured and difficult-to-evac patient, ran into some good luck. The Flight for Life chopper radioed to mission base that it was willing to land in the snowfield below us. We found the LZ to consist of highly consolidated snow that could safely support the weight of the air ambulance. This would reduce the length of our evac to just several pitches over a snow slope.

Even with the fortunate LZ location below us, I was concerned about the time. There was only about an hour of daylight left. Neither helicopter could operate in the mountains after sunset. Jim's group also had a bit of luck in that their victim's injuries allowed him to be transported to the road via Helicopter 185. Both evacs could continue in parallel, but the danger was increased by having two helicopters operating in the same narrow valley. Aerial coordination was imperative.

Jim picked an LZ approximately one thousand feet uphill from where his victim was located. This would require an uphaul to safely transport the boy up the hill in a litter. Jim's problem was to construct a complex hauling system and direct inexperienced rescuers to use it. Jim and his team got down to work.

This crescendo of rescue work portrayed mountain rescue at its most definitive. Two teams rising to the challenge of performing two simultaneous rescues, using all their physical and mental skills, as individuals and part of a team in the mountains. This is the pinnacle of a mountain rescuer's life: being in the wilderness, whether playing on a planned trip, or unexpectedly called to save lives, interrupting their daily routines to eagerly jump into a rescue full of unknowns. Everything is unique: the problems, solutions, locations, equipment, difficulties, disappointments, successes, rewards, and people. There is nothing like it in the world.

We were all in an intense rescue mode now, the kind that makes time race by unnoticed. My group was busy performing a downhill snow evac. We snugly packaged our victim and secured her in the litter. We rigged the rope for a scree evac and set up an equalized snow anchor using pickets, long metal bars hammered or buried in the snow to which the belay system is attached. The evac team descended Isabelle Glacier to where it flattened out enough for the chopper to set down. Lisa ran ahead with pickets to set up the next litter belay site. Ken Baugh belayed the litter as it was guided by two attendants rapidly down the slope. The team arrived at the LZ minutes later and only had to wait for the air ambulance to arrive. The increasing volume of its rhythmic thumping indicated it was rapidly approaching. The pilot asked for the GPS coordinates for the LZ. The rescuer I assigned to take coordinates had a GPS receiver failure as the ship approached. With no time to wait, I rifled through my pack for my GPS receiver, which was already turned on. The pilot wanted coordinates in degrees, minutes, and seconds, so I switched from UTM (Universal Transverse Mercator, a coordinate system used in navigation and available on maps and GPS receivers; UTM coordinates are measured in meters) coordinates, a system far more useful to hikers, and barked out the numbers. He confirmed, and Chuck followed with wind speed and direction at the LZ. We spotted the orange airship approaching high above the valley.

Below us about a half mile away, I could see Helicopter 185 on the ground waiting for Jim's victim. Its engine was off and the rotor made an unnatural-looking white X on the hilltop. Haulers and litter bearers labored downhill of the LZ to get the victim to the chopper. The tiny dots of the team were spread out over the slope in two clusters. One band of rescuers surrounded the litter, another stood in a line pulling on the haul rope. They were moving quickly.

Back at my site the air ambulance had arrived. The orange airship circled our location once, testing the wind conditions and observing the terrain. He touched down on the snow and signaled us to approach the ship. Six rescuers, ducking beneath the spinning rotor blades, carried the victim to the chopper and loaded her onboard. We retreated, ducking behind big rocks as the chopper lifted off, to protect ourselves in case the ship crashed back to the ground in the thin air. It lifted off without incident and sped out of sight.

I looked down toward the second mission site. Jim's group had their victim carefully loaded into Helicopter 185 for the short hop to the trailhead. I watched the chopper fly away looking down on it from above as it glided down the valley out of site. The boy was transferred to an ambulance at the trailhead.

I sent everyone down ahead of me, running sweep of the area, making sure no people or equipment were left behind. I listened to spirited end-of-mission radio chatter as I walked to the edge of the

LZ to an overlook at the top of a cliff face. The valley was in shadow and an evening humid chill had set in. I gazed out over Lake Isabelle and Long Lake in the distance, their blue water surfaces calm and clear. A small mountain brook was gurgling nearby, and I turned around and looked west to see a startlingly beautiful vision. The interplay of the evening sunlight and clouds around the peak summits was producing a double image, one solid and one a ghostly apparition, tracing out the real mountain in actual shape and size, but of curiously evanescent form. One image was a physical mountain, the other was an inspired projection. The display was a silent reminder of how the mountains inspire the intangible but profoundly real emotions of life.

My rescue radio snapped me back to reality. I was being called, asking for an estimated time of arrival at the trailhead. I said I'd be out in about an hour. I hiked down until I met Jim, who was also last to leave his rescue site. He excitedly described pulling off a mission with so many inexperienced rescuers, themselves ecstatic with the success. I described our mission, the helicopter flight, the difficult coordination problems, and solutions my team worked out. We trudged down in the darkness, stars shining brilliantly above us in the summer sky. We had both been up this trail uncounted times, so we needed no headlamps. Back at the trailhead, 1970 and two rescuers were waiting. I piled in and collapsed in the back seat, remaining silent as we returned to the shimmering town of Boulder below.

The First Diamond Evacuation

Longs Peak.
The Diamond is the
upper triangular face.
(Photo courtesy of Steve Poulsen)

LONGS PEAK IS ONE OF THE MOST renowned mountains in the United States. Rising to 14,255 feet above sea level, it is the higher of a dual-peak massif (the other peak being Mount Meeker at 13,911 feet). Its steep granite walls tower over the surrounding peaks as it stands like a giant sentinel overlooking northern Colorado. First described by explorer Major Stephen Long in 1820, it has been awe-inspiring to all who gaze upon it. Its summit has beckoned climbers from the beginning.

The steep cliffs surrounding the top of Longs thwarted early attempts at climbing the peak, but eventually a relatively easy route was found. The first confirmed summit happened in 1868 by a party lead by the seemingly incongruous pair of William Byers, founder and editor of the *Rocky Mountain News*, and John Wesley Powell, the famous one-armed explorer and Civil War veteran.

Since then, more than one hundred routes have been established on the peak. Currently thousands of people climb Longs each year, the vast majority via the Keyhole route, named for a keyhole-shaped portal on the northwest ridge. Unfortunately, this route leads the masses well away from a spectacular overlook called Chasm View, and so most miss an amazing panorama of the infamous East Face of Longs, a spectacular 1,600-foot alpine labyrinth of vast cliffs, huge ledges, and towering spires.

The East Face is bisected by a ledge called Broadway, 500 feet above the bottom of the face. Above Broadway towers the Diamond, a sheer, overhanging roughly diamond-shaped wall that rises over 1,000 feet from Broadway to just below the summit. When taking into account the technical difficulty, altitude, and climatic conditions, the climbing routes on the Diamond have the notorious claim of being the most difficult in the continental United States. The Diamond was "conquered" in August 1960 by David Rearick and Bob Kamps. Over two days, the pair made an ascent directly up the center of the face, a route they named "D1."

Rearick convinced Rocky Mountain National Park (RMNP) officials to allow them to climb by coming up with a 1,200-foot rope, supplied by mountaineering equipment guru Leroy Holubar, and providing two "support" teams in case they needed a rescue (see the section "Pioneers"). One team was on the mountain while the second team stayed in the shelter. After their success, they were recognized nationally as the most daring climbers in America. The Diamond was then wide open to climbers, attracting an ever-increasing number of ascensionists.

RMNP continued to use the model of requiring a "support" team for any climbers attempting the Diamond. This was a good idea, on paper. In practice, support teams mainly helped carry heavy loads of climbing gear to the start of the climb and officials asked few questions about rescue plans. As long as no rescues were actually necessary, this model worked well. As the number of climbers attempting the Diamond increased dramatically over the next few years, RMNP eliminated its rule requiring a support party. And as luck would have it, no one needed a rescue.

However, "it had become obvious that the time was fast approaching when a rescue from the Diamond would have to be done. It was also clear that teams from the Mountain Rescue Association (MRA) would have to do it," wrote now retired RMR member Jonathan Hough. The closest and most qualified groups were RMR and the Alpine Rescue Team. As the possibility of a rescue gestated, an idea was hatched to hold a practice evacuation off the Diamond face. It would be a pioneering effort: no vertical wall evac of that magnitude had ever been attempted before in the country. They initiated their planning for what would end up being a monumental exercise.

It was the weekend of August 16, 1969, when thirty RMR and six Alpine Rescue Team members gathered at the Longs Peak trailhead.

Coincidentally, the notorious Woodstock Music Festival was playing on the same weekend halfway across the country in New York State. (At Woodstock, Stephen Stills performed as part of his rock group Crosby, Stills, Nash and Young. A few years later, while living in Gold Hill, he would make a cameo appearance as an RMR volunteer.)

Instead of enjoying a psychedelic musical experience, this "party" at the base of Longs Peak loaded pack animals with 500 pounds of rescue gear, grabbed their personal packs, and headed up the trail. Their first stop was the Boulder Field, a descriptively named expanse located five miles and 3,000 feet above the trailhead at an altitude of 12,500 feet, the base of the upper slopes of Longs. This was as far as the pack animals could go, but not where the team would stop. The loads were then lugged on the backs of the rescuers another 1,500 feet up steep cliff faces until they were in position for the following day's event.

It had taken RMR much more than a difficult day of lugging gear to arrive at this point. "This was the culmination of several years of work to hone the techniques and mind-set of the group," Hough later recalled. "We'd been through a lot of practices at Eldo, Castle Rock, and elsewhere to push the envelope." They not only sharpened their skills and acquired the experience to do a big wall evac, but also obtained specialized equipment and precisely planned the logistical details of the exercise.

The rescuers bivouacked at 14,000 feet that night. Their plan was to start the evac at the crack of dawn to avoid dangerous afternoon thunderstorms. And they had planned well. Their rescue equipment list included:

> ...two 1,200 foot spools of climbing rope, another
> thousand or so feet of rope in shorter lengths, a Stokes
> litter, 50 odd pounds of hardware, bivouac gear, radios, and
> many peanut butter sandwiches.
>
> *Trail and Timberline*, March, 1970

This was a monumental undertaking that had never been attempted previously. The group was confident, but questions remained that could only be answered by doing the evac. It was known that the Diamond face was overhanging, but not by how much. When they arrived at the "victim," could they reach him or her? How much would a thousand feet of rope stretch when a victim was added to the litter?

And then there was the weather. Among the many potential climatic hazards, a lightning strike on the summit could be disastrous. Would the current travel down the nylon ropes? Or possibly up? In July 2001, a victim was killed by a lightning strike while climbing the Diamond. The deadly bolt of energy did not come from the sky, but out of the vertical face in front of the climber. This type of ground strike was not considered by the rescue team in 1969.

The rescuers attempted to get some sleep that night in their rocky perches. Sleeping at high altitude is problematic for the human body. The brain sometimes jolts a person awake gasping for air when sleep-induced hypoxia takes over. However, in general the rescuers felt OK, welcoming the rest after a long day of physical exertion. "I didn't have any problem the night before," recalled Hough. "We had to find bivouac places at the top of the Diamond for fifteen to twenty people. We found good ledges and caves; it was an unexpected bonus."

The next morning dawned in good weather. Dave Pahlke had bivouacked well below the summit on the Broadway ledge. That morning he climbed up the Diamond and positioned himself as a "victim" on the wall, about 800 feet from the top. Dave Lewis was positioned as a spotter on Mount Lady Washington, a perfect vantage point directly across from the Diamond.

An anchor was built around the massive boulders near the summit. The litter was constructed and rigged to the ropes. Dave communicated with the evac team as to which takeoff point would best align with the victim. It would be difficult to load the victim if the litter was too far out of vertical alignment. The brakes were threaded. The system was double-checked. Everything was set.

Hough and Harvey Mastalir were to be the litter bearers. The litter was tied into dual 1,200-foot Goldline ropes, still wound on the original manufacturer's spools. Hough and Mastalir tied in to the litter and muscled it to the edge of the face.

"We instantly had about 2,000 feet of exposure," Hough recalled. "Stepping over a 2,000-foot ledge is something very few people experience. Some people may be upset, nervous, or scared. For me it wasn't that way. It was pleasant and comfortable to be back in that vertical world." Hough was a hard-core rock climber, and having climbed the Diamond years before, he was on familiar ground.

There wasn't much for Hough and Mastalir to do but enjoy the ride down for the next 800 feet. They were now relying not only on the lowering crew but also their gear to work as planned, much as a test pilot relies on his experimental airplane to work. But Hough and Mastalir had no way to eject and float away from crashing hardware.

A problem developed almost immediately. Kinks were forming in the ropes above the brake plate. When they were first noticed, they seemed minor but very quickly threatened to jam up the brake system, halting any motion at all, and thus rendering the litter and its bearers hanging motionless on the face.

The two ropes were being fed directly off of the original spools they were wound on when manufactured. The lowering crew quickly solved the problem. They realized the only way to relieve the twist was to pick up and manually turn the heavy spools. A crew formed to spin the awkward 86-pound masses as the litter descended. Over the course of the evac the spools were lifted and turned over an estimated one thousand times. It was a monstrous physical workout for those on the top and slowed the litter's descent rate to a crawl.

As the crew at the top heaved the spools around, the litter bearers "hung out" with nothing much to do. At one point Mastalir pulled out a harmonica (he had the forethought to carry one) and played as Hough held his radio microphone open as "entertainment for the lowering crew."

The minutes passed as they slowly descended the vertiginous wall. The weather was holding and no other major problems surfaced. Spotter Lewis reported by radio the relative positions of litter and "victim" on the giant vertical landscape. They finally arrived at Pahlke, their "victim." It was now the litter bearers' time to work. They would have to move Pahlke from the wall to the litter without the help of a "third-man." The third-man is a third rescuer independent of the litter system, usually rappelling on his own rope, who assists the litter bearers with the difficult job of safely and carefully removing a victim from the wall and into the litter. The impracticalities of this technique on the Diamond required the litter bearers to do the job alone.

Hough and Mastalir were highly experienced in vertical loading techniques. Hough recalled few problems loading the victim. They did, however, have to deal with greater than usual rope stretch. Goldline is highly dynamic, or stretchable, rope. The longer the rope is, the more it will stretch when a load is put on it. If a 200-pound victim jumped onto the litter hanging on 800 feet of rope, both would drop uncontrollably for dozens of feet before the bungee effect bounced them to a stop. A victim must be "lowered" into a litter, adding weight slowly as the ropes stretch. Hough and Mastalir were able to manage the problem and soon Pahlke was successfully strapped in, and they were on their way down. A major milestone had been achieved.

Very soon after, they arrived at Broadway where they could stand on horizontal ground again. But their goal was still 500 feet below, the base of the East Face. They struggled to get the litter across the ledge system, having to pull the litter away from the wall dozens of feet as they walked down to the next edge, dealing with the rubber-band effect of the ropes while trying to coordinate with the lowering crew over the radio. They finally reached the edge and down they went uneventfully to the ground. Success! It had taken them a total of one hour and 46 minutes. They were about 1,600 feet down from the top, but still on their 1,200-foot ropes. The ropes stretched the extra 400 feet.

Rocky Mountain Rescue had demonstrated the feasibility of rescuing a disabled party on the Diamond, the most difficult big wall in the country. Their demonstration showed a victim could be rescued safely and efficiently by a highly trained volunteer mountain rescue team. It had never been done, and was a historical event in mountain rescue, another first from RMR. While the exercise was actually only a minor technical advancement, a major psychological barrier was crossed. Big-wall rescue in Colorado was now a reality.

Hough recalled the glorious day: "I was happy we achieved a hallmark for the group and mountain rescue in general, and wished it would have gone on longer."

Autumn

*"2 backcountry skiers caught,
1 buried and killed."*

COLORADO AVALANCHE INFORMATION CENTER
ACCIDENT REPORT

YANKEE DOODLE LAKE
NOVEMBER 28, 2001

Mutual
Aid

*David Syring's body being
evacuated from a snow-
covered Mount Lindsey.*
(Photo courtesy of Paul Woodword)

THE FLIGHT TOOK APPROXIMATELY ONE HOUR. The lightweight and powerful Lama helicopter streaked south along the Front Range mountains of Colorado carrying a crew consisting of a pilot and two mountain rescuers. They could see for hundreds of miles through the clear blue sky. They glided above the rock faces of Mount Evans, Mount Bierstadt, and Pikes Peak. They then soared over the jagged spires and steep, snow-covered peaks of the far-flung and isolated Sangre de Cristo mountains.

They soon approached Mount Lindsey in the wild, sparsely populated southern edge of Colorado. It is a giant, standing over 14,000 feet above sea level, with three cardinal flanks guarded by smaller peaks. Lindsey's sister mountain, the mighty Blanca Peak, lies on Lindsey's western flank, connected to it via a cliffbound ridge far above timberline. The rescuers recognized this wild and remote terrain, though they had never seen it from this god's-eye view. It reminded them of the difficult work they performed here in the last few weeks, and hopefully their job could be completed today with the use of this high-tech flying machine. The pilot steered the helicopter over a rocky saddle and into the basin north of Lindsey's summit.

In the weeks prior, a team of mountain rescuers had marked the location where the helicopter would land as best it could, but new snow driven by incessant wind had covered their flagging. The pilot hovered low and slow over the ground while the rescuers searched. Someone spotted a small patch of red surveyor's tape poking out of the white snow. The pilot hovered and then touched down in the rocky basin, and the rescuers jumped out into the sharply cold air. They were there to finally pick up the body of David Syring, an experienced fifty-eight-year-old hiker who fell to his death on the last 14,000-foot peak he had yet to climb in Colorado.

This mission began weeks before. RMR was paged out on a Sunday night in early October to help in a search for a missing climber on Mount Lindsey, one of the higher peaks in Colorado and a popular hiking destination. Mount Lindsey happens to be located in Costilla County in south-central Colorado. This is a sparsely populated region that relies on mutual aid for mountain rescue. Just as RMR depends on neighboring mountain rescue groups to supply personnel for difficult or protracted missions in Boulder County, RMR members help other teams with rescues around the state. Four of us volunteered to make last-minute changes to our plans and take a day off work on Monday and help with the search.

Ken Baugh, Steve Poulsen, "Big John" Snyder, and I met at 4 A.M. at RMR's equipment cache. We picked up the gear we thought would be useful and embarked on the four-hour drive south to the small town of Gardner, where we would meet up with the sheriff of Costilla County and other mountain rescuers from around the state. When we finally arrived, groggy from the early rise and long drive, we saw that about 20 rescuers were gathered. A sheriff's deputy began the debriefing.

On September 30, a pair of hikers reported they had seen a body. They believed it was the body of another hiker whom they had spoken to earlier that day during a break, an older man who was solo-climbing the peak. The man was ascending the same route and after a brief conversation, the man continued his ascent ahead of the RPs and disappeared around a rock outcropping.

Several minutes later, the RPs reported hearing a rockslide. They weren't overly concerned since spontaneous rockfall is rather common on that loose section of the peak. The pair continued their climb. They did a traversing ascent of a steep slope that was covered with loose, icy rock. This was a tricky and somewhat dangerous section of an otherwise easy climb. The RPs finally attained the highest ridge and arrived on the summit a few minutes later.

They were somewhat baffled by the absence of the man ahead of them. Maybe he had summitted and descended a different route? It was possible but not likely, since any other descent route would be more circuitous and difficult. It was possible that the man descended below the summit ridge slightly and they passed him at some point. This was also not likely since the weather was perfect and the route not complicated. The pair started their descent, somewhat concerned about the welfare of this other hiker. As they descended from the summit ridge to the tricky loose section, one of the pair fell.

He was able to stop his fall, suffering only minor scrapes and bruises. During his fall, many rocks were knocked loose and tumbled down the couloir, creating a stone avalanche. When he recovered somewhat and looked around to assess his position, he was horrified to see a body lying on the slope below him. The body was lying head-up, facedown in the couloir, arms outstretched as if to stop his slide, and covered in rocks. Having already survived a mishap and certain the person was dead, the pair wisely decided to retreat off of the slope and report what they saw. They suspected the body was that of the older man they had seen but were not positive. When the sheriff got the news, he knew he needed mountain rescue help. Costilla County, its small population spread out over a large area, had no way to organize a large group of experienced mountaineers on its own. The call went out for help to the numerous volunteer mountain rescue teams in the state.

By the time the conglomerated rescue team, made up of personnel from the far-flung corners of the state, was debriefed that morning, the RPs were long gone. We had to rely on a report based on interviews conducted the day before. The report had not really focused on the details that would help us find the body but did contain a general description that would point us in the right direction. We knew all the climbers were on the standard ascent route and near the summit. The entire team finally left for the trailhead about 30 miles away. Steve, John, Ken, and I drove to the trailhead in John's 4x4 truck. When we arrived at the trailhead staging area, we met a group from Western State Mountain Rescue Team, a young team based out of Western State College in Gunnison. They were short on experience, but full of energy and enthusiasm and had laid out a tarp on which they were unloading and sorting gear.

We discussed a plan. It turned out that I was the only person who had climbed Mount Lindsey previously, so I became the "guide," though the route up the peak was easy to follow. I led a light and hasty team to attempt to find the exact location of the body and direct the shortest route for the heavy evacuation gear brought in on the backs of the majority of the rescuers there. Being the hasty team guide was one of the better jobs to have, but I always appreciated that the work could not be done without the efforts of the much larger group doing the dirty work of carrying the heavy gear, some of which added 50 pounds to their required personal gear.

Steve, a Western State rescuer, and I bolted up the trail with a couple of ropes, radios, and personal climbing gear. Someone from Western State would remain at the trailhead and provide mission base support. Ken and "Big John" led the team humping the loads up the trail.

The pace of our hasty team was tough, and I was feeling the effects of lack of sleep, a junk food breakfast, and the funk that comes from being trapped in a car listening to Ken's incessant bad jokes for four hours. But the suffering was tolerable; it was a beautiful day for a hike. As with many autumn days in the Colorado Rockies, it was neither too hot nor too cold. The air was strikingly clear and calm, with a hint of the brisk smell of the approaching winter. The aspen trees were in full color, painting the mountainsides with radiant yellow and orange patches in the early afternoon sunlight. We would enjoy nature as fully as possible on our hike in, knowing that a grim scene awaited us above.

After two hours at a fast pace, I asked Steve to do a radio check with the team following us. I estimated the main group was about 45 minutes behind, slowed down with their heavy burden of evacuation equipment. They had stopped for a short rest and we did as well. We were slowing down due to the sparsity of oxygen at this altitude. I sat down and took several gulps of water. A light breeze chilled my sweat-soaked shirt, but I didn't waste time putting on a jacket; we would be back at work hiking soon.

We were far above timberline at 13,100 feet and could now see the upper north slopes of the mountain where the route gets more difficult. The RPs reported the body was in the second of three major couloirs on the north face of Mount Lindsey. From our vantage point we counted five major couloirs. We decided to follow the normal route and search intersecting couloirs.

The route climbed up the first couloir before traversing left and out higher on the face. There was no body in this couloir, but it did present more of a challenge than the hiking we were doing previously. The couloir was steep and required scrambling techniques, easy hand-over-hand climbing. Recent snowfall had iced up the holds so that careful climbing was required. One could easily imagine a misstep here resulting in a serious fall down the slope. At the top of this section we followed the easy traverse to the next couloir.

We looked down and saw a human shape about 200 feet below us in the middle of the second couloir. Steve hiked down a rocky rib forming the near side of the couloir to get a closer look. The body had several head-sized rocks piled on top of it. If the fall hadn't immediately killed him, the subsequent rockslide that he set off did.

He was wearing old-style wool knickers and a flannel shirt, perfectly appropriate fabrics but decades out of style. He looked like a dauntless mountaineer of old, an ancient breed of hikers who had begun their vocation back when it was strange and rare. This was his ending, perhaps one misstep in the one-hundred thousand steps he'd hiked, or perhaps his last step was as perfect as those prior, but his luck ran out while stepping on a rock that had held in place for a thousand years, but gave way that instant.

His outstretched arms told a tale of struggle in the last seconds of his life. One could imagine his horror of finding himself suddenly and unexpectedly sliding down this loose, rocky chute, desperately gripping at whatever rock feature was near, only to find himself sliding too fast, his body generating a force too much for his fingers to bear, but relentlessly and frantically gripping until his fingertips broke off and lower knuckles pulled out of their sockets. The force of his fall against the face pulled larger rocks down on top of him. The shower of rocks pummeled him to unconsciousness and death. It appeared to have happened very quickly.

But this was David's fate, turning what was surely a fun hike on an easy mountain into the end of his life. I looked down at his broken body. He had climbed for many years and I am sure had gotten the same feelings of enjoyment and fulfillment that I feel when I climb. His death was sudden and tragic, yet as death is also part of life, death in the mountains is a part of many mountaineers' lives. There have been times in my own mountaineering career in which I've balanced on the very edge of life in dangerous situations, acutely aware of each moment and movement I've made. There have been other times when I was on that precarious edge of life but did not recognize it until later.

But most of the time I've spent in the mountains has been far from that edge, and surely David did not feel near that precipice either.

We radioed the main part of the group and had them hold at the saddle, about 800 feet below us. We needed to evaluate the situation and only have the necessary gear for an evac brought up to our level. I observed the couloir for about five minutes and saw several spontaneous rock falls directly down the couloir, probably hitting the body. The freeze/thaw cycle of the new snow turning to water then ice was causing the already extremely loose rock in the couloir to shower down without warning.

Extracting the body via a scree evac down or an uphaul out would require many rescuers to spend hours in this couloir, exposing us to certain injury by rockfall. After consultation with the main part of the team, we decided that the danger was too great to attempt a conventional extraction. The victim was dead, and we were not going to make matters worse by allowing one of us to be injured or killed.

We retreated and regrouped with the other twenty-five rescuers but had a dilemma on our hands. Could we ever retrieve this victim in a safe manner? A helicopter might be able to do it, but it would require hovering at nearly 14,000 feet. This takes a lot of power that most choppers do not have. Some military choppers could do this job, but there would remain the problem of rotor wash knocking down more rocks on whomever was below, so that probably wasn't the answer.

The rescue team descended to the trailhead in the fading daylight. We reported to the sheriff the dangerous position of the body and our inability to retrieve it under current conditions. I thought of waiting for a significant snowfall that would certainly happen soon in the rapidly approaching winter. The rocks would be buried and cemented into place, rendering the gully safe from rockfall. Of course, with significant snowfall, avalanches become the new objective danger. Objective dangers are hazards out of rescuers' control. No one wanted to leave a body on the mountain. It was along a popular climbing route, and the family of the victim would be understandably upset. But there was nothing to be done for the moment.

The family of the victim was immensely frustrated and looked to whatever resources they could. The day after our initial efforts at recovery, they enlisted a team of Special Forces soldiers from nearby Fort Carson. David was a Green Beret who had served in Vietnam and so the Special Forces team was more than happy to try their hand at recovery. Their attempt was thwarted by newly fallen snow and their inability to deal with environmental conditions.

We mountain rescuers knew from our initial attempt that there would be a time in the not too distant future when it would be possible to attempt an extraction in relative safety. The family's action of searching for a more professional rescue team illustrates a misconception about volunteer mountain rescue teams. The word "volunteer" implies "amateur," as if members are just dabbling in a hobby. Somehow, paying money for a "professional" team implies the members would be better suited for the tough missions. This fallacy is pointedly illustrated by this mission. Only the volunteers who put in hundreds of hours of training year after year, and who participate in many rescues, have the highest level of knowledge and skill to perform these tasks.

Snow accumulated in the high mountains over the next few weeks. If this couloir was blanketed with enough snow (as reported by the military rescuers), the spontaneous rockfall would be eliminated. The avalanche conditions could be evaluated, predicted, and perhaps mitigated by triggering a slide. The deep snow, cold, and lack of daylight in winter would of course make the approach and evacuation far more difficult. But at least the couloir might be safer. The physical difficulties could be overcome with hard work.

Alpine Rescue Team (ART) led the third effort. Paul "Woody" Woodward called me at work one afternoon and asked for detailed information as to the body location and couloir condition. We spoke for two hours as I described the scene. I told him of my theory that the right amount of snow would make it safe. Several of ART's members went down to the site where Woody and Mike Everist found the body in the same state as it was weeks before, only now covered with a moderate layer of snow.

They were able to evacuate it in relative safety down the couloir to the bottom of the north face, just as predicted. There was a good balance of snow, enough to glue the rocks in place but not present a serious avalanche threat.

They ran out of daylight as the evac proceeded. They brought the body to a good flat area and packaged the victim in layered body bags. They added red surveyor tape so it could be easily seen in the vast rock and snow basin by the next team.

Woody talked with the family and, through many days of negotiations and official wrangling, eventually arranged for a private Lama helicopter to fly Ken and him from Denver to Mount Lindsey, where they would pick up the body and fly it back to Denver and David's family.

Woody, Ken, and the helicopter pilot met at Centennial Airport south of Denver on a clear November morning. All three donned their crash helmets and strapped in. A Lama is a small but powerful helicopter perfect for flying at high altitudes. The National Park Service in Denali National Park uses a stripped-down Lama to perform rescues at extreme altitudes (and for extreme dollar cost) near the summit of Mount McKinley. It was perfect for this mission.

Ken and Woody were now back in the basin below the north face of Mount Lindsey after their spectacular tour of the front range, having found the red-flagged body that Woody had packaged a week before. They were here to complete the job of removing a mountaineering accident victim's body from the mountains, a feat that was completed by the determination of experienced volunteer teams.

They were at about 12,000 feet and the wind chill from the chopper froze their faces and hands. The pilot kept the engine going so he could maintain control if a rogue wind gust threatened to blow the chopper on its side. Ken and Woody uncovered the body and carried it to the ship. They strapped the body on the skid litter and jumped back on ship.

The Lama was able to lift off with the added weight. They retraced their route out of the mountains over the newly snow-covered slopes. Ken and Woody slowly warmed up in the unheated chopper as they returned through the dazzling mountain scenery to Centennial Airport and the waiting family.

The family was immensely thankful. The stress, frustration, and helpless feelings over the last month were finished. They had agonized over the lack of closure, having their loved one's body stuck on a remote, inaccessible mountain slope.

When the body was unloaded, David's son and brother were waiting. They experienced their catharsis by witnessing the return of the body and touching the body through the bag. It's difficult to imagine what "lack of closure" means until it is experienced. The life of the beloved family member is suddenly and surprisingly taken away. It is not planned or even thought of until it impacts like a meteor strike in the pastoral landscape of their lives. It is rewound and experienced over and over in the mind and soul until the sadness and loss fade to a tolerable level. But it is a disaster that cannot be completely resolved without the final task of burying the dead. Today it was finally finished, and life could go on for them.

Ken and Woody were able to comfort the family only in a limited way for the great loss that was once again being brought to the surface for them. But they had finished the job, which took weeks and scores of rescuers doing long, cold, backbreaking work.

They were thrilled by the flight, exhausted by the freezing and difficult high-altitude work, and saddened by witnessing the loss of another family's loved one, all in the span of a single day. They now felt exhaustion. They headed out to get a bite to eat, try to calm their minds, and get some rest that night, and like all volunteer rescuers, lumber into their real jobs the next morning. Life goes on for the rescuer, too.

Eye of the Needle

Rescuers examine debris one day after Yankee Doodle Lake avalanche. Ice chunks filled lake below.
(Photo courtesy of Jeff Sparhawk)

IT WAS NOVEMBER 28, 2001, at 11,000 feet above sea level in the pine-speckled mountains west of Boulder. The sun had the severity of white fire. The naked eye recoiled in sharp pain as the muscles of the iris frantically contracted, squeezing the round pupil as tightly as possible, like looking into a car headlight from a distance of a few inches. Sunglasses were required. A moderate zephyr flowed from the west, chilling the air just enough to require a wind-deflecting jacket. A better-than-average autumn day in Colorado.

It was the grand opening of backcountry ski season. It had been cold enough in the mountains to hold permanent snow for the last two months, but the dry Colorado climate is stingy with snowstorms. The snow that does fall will not melt, but it takes a couple of months to accumulate a skiable layer. The layer was now in, and like surfers who wait months in anticipation of giant winter waves at Waimea Bay, backcountry skiers in Boulder could relish in the sport they'd impatiently waited for all summer.

Twenty-nine-year-old Joe Despres was having fun. He and his ski partner, forty-seven-year-old Peter Vaughn were on their third day of a skiing rampage. Joe was athletic and loved being in the mountains for whatever reason: hiking, mountain biking, or skiing. He and his passion for outdoor sports were both born on the East Coast, where he participated in many water sports.

The rumor was that at some point he decided he wanted a change in lifestyle because he sharply reduced his participation in water sports. He was bothered by recurrent dreams of disaster in the water, where he faced a watery death. He was bothered so much by what he felt was an ominous warning that he eventually moved to Nederland, Colorado, where he continued his love of physical activity and outdoor sports far from the ocean.

Today, he and Peter were standing at the top of their challenge, ready to go for the adrenaline rush of flying down a snowfield, turning and gliding with well-honed skills to control their descent, carving artistic waving curves on the 45-degree slope. The had prepared for the known dangers. They dug a snowpit to the ground to view the layers of snow. Storms that pass through deposit snow in layers, and thermodynamic processes change those layers over time. They examined each striation, looking for a weak point. They found none today. And they had found none the previous two days, this was their third day in a row skiing the same incredibly fun slope. Just in case, they also wore avalanche beacons, which they checked for operability before their descent.

It was 1 P.M., the checklist was complete, and now was the time to go for it.

At 4 P.M. down in the flatlands north of the city of Boulder, I was driving down Foothills Highway as the late autumn sun dropped below the western mountains. The west wind buffeted my car as I drove north under cobalt blue skies. My rescue pager crackled to life. "Rocky Mountain Rescue, stage at the Eldora Ski Area to search for a victim caught in an avalanche." I turned my car around and started the drive up the mountains to the ski area. I knew it would be dark when I arrived.

As I drove up Boulder Canyon, I turned on my radio to get the details. There was an avalanche reported at Yankee Doodle Lake. Yankee Doodle is a small, high-altitude lake located several miles west of the ski area and below the Needle Eye Tunnel near the Continental Divide. Access to the lake is difficult. During the summer you must drive 10 miles along a rough dirt road along an old railroad grade. The road is not plowed in winter, underscoring its isolation. I arrived at the town of Nederland and followed the meandering shelf road to the ski area. I arrived at dusk just as a helicopter was touching down. Jeff Sparhawk, an RMR member with an avalanche-qualified search dog, was just about ready and asked me to check the functionality of his avalanche beacon. He and his dog, Kiyla, got on board and lifted off. There were about 30 rescuers staging in the dark parking area, getting prepared in the cold wind whooshing down Bryan Mountain.

I made my way to the ski patrol shack, where I heard a terrifying and amazing story. A haggard man came staggering down the slopes of the ski area late that afternoon. He was wearing thin clothing completely inappropriate for the cold and windy conditions. He was wearing telemark ski boots but had no skis, he was running through the clumsy snow. He ran to the patrol shack where he was recognized. The shivering and exhausted man was Peter Vaughn, another Eldora ski patroller. His voice shook as he frantically told the Eldora ski patrollers he and Joe were caught in an avalanche five miles west of there near Needle Eye Tunnel. He had lost all of his gear. He could not find Joe.

I then heard radio traffic in the growing chaos of the patrol shack. The helicopter reported the avalanche path to be 300 feet wide and 1,000 feet long. A hasty team was already on the scene, searching with transceivers and dogs. There wasn't much daylight left. Though they were able to put a hasty team in, the helicopter was no longer able to fly in the area due to the darkness and wind.

Someone announced there were snowplows trying to get through the Needle Eye Tunnel road, so I jumped in "Big John" Snyder's ever present and utilitarian 4x4 truck, and we drove 45 minutes down from the ski area to the next valley south by Moffat Tunnel. We rapidly caught up with and followed the caravan of vehicles for several miles along a dirt road. Big snowplows demolished the few large drifts in a road surprisingly free of snow. We finally arrived at the lake and were astonished by the scene.

It was completely dark with a bone-chilling wind howling from the west. We were just below timberline standing at the edge of a frozen lake about 300 feet wide. The far end of the lake was a jumbled mess of humongous snow chunks. The avalanche path on the slope above was lit up by powerful spotlights, illuminating it like a phantom mountain glowing in the dark. Several small black figures could be seen frantically searching the slopes and debris below. In the darkness I could see the pinpoint flashing LED lights on avalanche transceivers of the searchers. The lake surface was a frozen jumble of broken icebergs. The wide, thick slab of dense snow that became the avalanche had broken free from far above and driven itself into the lake with thunderous force. The powerful surge of snow broke through the two-foot-thick layer of surface ice. Tons of snow injected itself into the lake, triggering a 12-foot tsunami of water and large ice chunks that ravaged around the shores, scouring them of snow but depositing ice chunks high on the shore. The air was so cold that the lake surface had refrozen solid within hours, suspending ice chunks the size of Volkswagens on the surface so that it looked like the scattered bones of a horrible ice monster.

The avalanche was triggered during Joe and Peter's descent earlier that day. Peter had skied down first. He stopped at a rock outcropping about halfway down to watch Joe. As Joe started, a gigantic slab of wind-hardened snow gave way beneath him. The slab quickly broke up and turned into a raging frozen river. It appeared as if the entire mountain was moving, the kind of scene that produces a reptilian fear response, a deep, sickening vertigo. Both men were now subject to nature's forces; nothing could be done. The snow torrent quickly overtook Peter and shoved him down the slope ahead of Joe. They both tumbled and rode the cold, white chaos for several hundred feet until they hit Yankee Doodle Lake.

Peter was pushed 200 feet from shore, where he ended up in water, floating in a riotously wavy sea of large ice blocks, still underneath a thick layer of snow. He rode haplessly in the swooshing water, avoiding the potentially body crushing icebergs until the wave action melted the snow layer above him. When he came to his senses, Peter could now realize where he was. His skis were gone. He removed his pack and put it on one of the ice chunks. He then swam his way through the freezing water to shore. He removed his soaked outer layer of clothing and looked for Joe. Peter frantically searched the avalanche debris for 45 minutes, listening for Joe's beacon signal but heard nothing. Finally, his survival mode kicked in and Peter ran five miles back to the Eldora ski area with very little clothing and no over-snow equipment. He limped into the first-aid station, hypothermic from his ordeal but showing a superhuman drive to survive.

Several hours had passed before the majority of rescuers arrived at the site. The chances of Joe surviving were nil. Nevertheless, the search was carried out as if Joe were still alive. No trace of Joe was found in the avalanche debris above the lake. I had walked to the far shore of the lake and found Peter's frozen outer shell of clothing he had stripped out of earlier. We could see Peter's pack sitting on an ice chunk in the lake. Eventually, a rescuer with a special ice rescue suit went out onto the lake to do a beacon search. He picked up a faint signal and homed in on it. Joe's body was found around midnight. He was frozen under the ice 90 feet from shore, just out of range of land-based beacon receivers.

The next day several RMR members accompanied Dale Atkins, avalanche forecaster for the Colorado Avalanche Information Center, to the site. We hiked up to the fracture line and watched as Dale examined the layers of snow. We stood below the fracture where the slab had broken, a five-foot wall of striated snow. Dale discovered a layer of "sugar snow" near the bottom part of the fracture wall. That layer was the weakness in the snowpack; all the snow above that layer broke free when Joe hit an unseen and undetectable weak spot. Peter and Joe were experts, but had missed this clue even though they had dug a snowpit.

A relatively high number of avalanche deaths occur in Colorado every year, and tragically Joe had become one of those statistics. There were some unusual aspects of this accident, however. The fact that Joe and Peter had taken every precaution, as in digging a snow pit and observing weather patterns, and had skied this slope the two prior days without incident, are unusual precursors to an avalanche accident. But possibly the most chilling aspect of this accident was the manner of Joe's death. Trauma and suffocation are the usual causes of death in an avalanche—the snow usually rakes and twists your body in the torrent and then leaves you buried in a cement-like grave with no air. Joe's cause of death was strangely different. Despite having escaped from the ocean, he wasn't able to avoid the fate foretold in his dreams. It was determined that Joe had water in his lungs. He died by drowning, far from his coastal homeland.

Mission Completed

Vertical evacuation.
(Photo courtesy of Jeff Sparhawk)

"There is a whole angle of rescue that is institutionally downplayed, and that is the danger [of mountain rescue work] ... I think that it's part of the image of the rescuer, to show strength and resolve and character and capacity. And it's part of the volunteer ethic that you don't dwell on the danger image. And you don't want to talk about it all the time but you don't want to ignore it completely; it's not healthy."

Jonathan Hough, RMR Group Leader 1963

"The reason I joined RMR was that it is an extremely competent organization which was 'playing for real.' It's one thing to join a checkers club, but quite another to join an organization making decisions about life and death. We can't make mistakes. We have to be competent 'or else.' RMR has an incredible safety record. I think it stems from our obsession with competence and uncompromising independence."

Chuck Demarest, RMR Group Leader 1968–1969

DANGER AND RISK ARE FACTS OF LIFE. When participating in the sport of mountaineering, the difference between a close call and a debilitating accident is a very thin, harsh line. Remain on one side of the line and life goes on as usual; the other side is injury, both physical and psychological, which radically changes life for the worse.

147

Understanding this danger drives Rocky Mountain Rescue to "do things right." RMR's safety record is the result of understanding the essential nature of mountain rescue work. Scott Whitehead, a long-time mountain rescuer, has an oft-repeated mantra: "RMR likes to make rescue boring." He means that we want to do it by the book, try to take the excitement of the unknown out of the equation. No flamboyant actions, no batman rescues, do what we've done before, avoid inventing something new on a mission unless absolutely necessary. The result is RMR has had no serious mission accident during its six decades of existence. More than one thousand different members have performed several thousand missions during this time.

We pick up the pieces of a broken body at the bottom of a cliff. If luck prevails, the victim is alive and we perform immediate medical procedures in dark, open-air, vertical walls with rain pouring down. We struggle for hours to move the victim down steep, rocky, snowy ground as quickly as possible. We then repack our ropes, count our carabiners, write off the blood-soaked personal jacket that we put on a victim, and scrub the body fluid stains off of the litter.

IT IS A CRISP OCTOBER NIGHT under fiercely twinkling stars. We are finally approaching the trailhead as evidenced by bright lights shining through the trees. A TV news camera and reporters are taking pictures as we come into view. Every one of us is dirty and unkempt as we clumsily maneuver the litter. The better-than-perfect appearance of the TV reporter primping for a live shot is a stark, almost comical contrast. We walk to the back of the ambulance and turn the litter for loading. We strap the litter to a pram and transfer our patient to the back of the ambulance. It is chilly out, but I am soaked in sweat due to the physical labor of the last few hours. The cool air feels good as I walk back toward 1970 with a brake plate.

Many group members are gathered around the brightly lit circle around the truck like friends gathered around a campfire. Everyone is busy coiling ropes, reassembling bash kits, stashing PI'ed (poison ivy contaminated) equipment into trashbags, and checking off gear lists. The rescue radio is loud in the background; it is very busy with traffic from the fire departments, sheriff, park rangers, ambulance, and RMR. The critical part of the mission is over and everyone is tying up loose ends. All RMR members are in from the field and accounted for.

We talk excitedly about our strenuous evac. There are smiles all around and much laughter as someone describes how they clumsily fell off the trail into a ravine. He wasn't hurt and it looked like a comedy act. He was especially skillful in letting go of the litter as he went down so as to not drag everyone down with him. Everyone is anxious about washing soon; we trampled through dying but dense poison ivy on this mission.

We all missed dinner, and so the Salvation Army has brought us sandwiches, chips, and drinks. Though not a gourmet meal, it tastes better than any meal I can remember. Some eat ravenously and go for seconds. More joking about how hard the work was and ribbing about who was slacking off. I hear some talk about climbing a mountain somewhere in Colorado next weekend. One person says, with some gleeful satisfaction, he is going to be late for work tomorrow. He'll have a good excuse.

All of the gear is repacked and 1970 is ready to go. Most people have left now, going home to collapse into bed. I walk the short distance to my car and open the back door. I take off my pack and throw it in the back. Most of my personal gear will need to be repacked and restocked. My headlamp batteries need to be replaced. Need to put a spare water bottle in the car. But I will do that tomorrow.

The feeling I have as I drive away is of great satisfaction. I am physically spent, but it is the kind of tiredness that you get at the end of a good, hard workout. I'm no longer hungry or thirsty. I have just spent several hours in the mountains I love, with many friends, all working together. And we saved a life.

Years ago when I came upon those hurt and dying mountain climbers on the high peaks of Colorado, I had no idea how or even if they could be saved. I only knew that I wanted to help rescue them if possible. I could only guess at what direction a vocation in mountain rescue would take me, and I would have guessed wrong.

Over the years, RMR has made me experience intensely difficult physical work and mental stress. I've made lasting friendships through tough missions and backcountry vacations. I've enjoyed the beauty of mountain sunsets on warm and windless summer evenings while walking to the trailhead after a save. I've fought freezing wind and blowing ice at 4 A.M. in a desolate wilderness, knowing that we lost someone. I've been through the trial by fire, dealing with death and massive bodily injuries caused by accidents, but learned how to provide treatment and quickly evacuate victims to a lifesaving hospital.

The years of training, the technical problem solving, and working with danger have paid off. The constant back-wrenching work of mountain rescue—hauling loads up a mountain and then carrying an injured human down to be restored to life—generates a profound feeling. It is better than I expected; this cannot come from anywhere else in life. I will be reminded of this good feeling for many days, and this good feeling in turn will be remembered forever. This is what RMR is about.

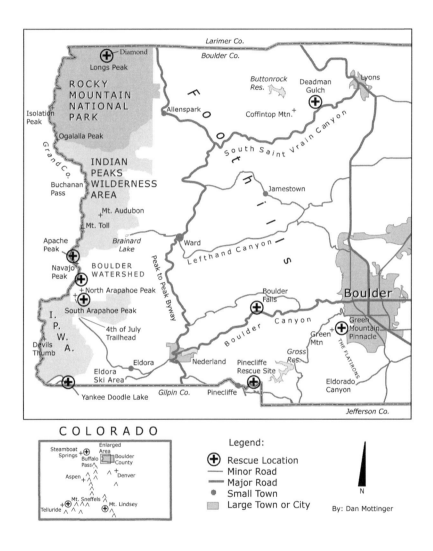

The Group Leader, or GL, of RMR is the person responsible for the operational readiness of the group. The GL is elected to a one-year term and is the official leader and spokesman for the group.

1947	Charles Hutchinson	1975	Walt Fricke
1948	Charles Hutchinson	1976	Lewis Dahm
1949	Dexter Brinker	1977	Dean Bowyer
1950	Brad Beisler, Wes Horner, John Houston; Dave Rose	1978	Dean Bowyer
		1979	Walt Fricke
1951	Dexter Brinker	1980	Lewis Dahm
1952	Tom Hornbein, Harry Waldrop, Harold Walton	1981	Lewis Dahm
		1982	Bruce Bartram
1953	Al Kempers, Harold Walton	1983	Bruce Bartram
		1984	Bruce Bartram
1954	Bob Sutton, John Clark	1985	Ray Sundby
1955	Raymond Batson	1986	Ray Sundby
1957	Willie Colony, Dave Lewis	1987	Ray Sundby
		1988	Ray Sundby
1958	Dave Lewis, Rich Schaefer	1989	Dixon Hutchinson
1959	Rich Schaefer, Tom Neilsen	1990	Dixon Hutchinson
		1991	Scott Whitehead
1960	Ed Anderson	1992	Scott Whitehead
1961	Dave Lewis	1993	Ted Krieger
1962	Dave Lewis	1994	Ted Krieger
1963	Jonathan Hough, Charlie Roskosz (briefly)	1995	Jenny Paddock
		1996	Jenny Paddock
1964	Asa Ramsay	1997	Jenny Paddock
1965	Asa Ramsay	1998	Ted Krieger
1966	Mark Ryan	1999	Rik Henrikson
1967	Rod Smythe	2000	Rik Henrikson
1968	Chuck Demarest	2001	Kevin Harner
1969	Chuck Demarest	2002	Jeff Sparhawk
1970	Joe Stepanek	2003	Jonathan Horne
1971	Bill May	2004	Jonathan Horne
1972	Bill May	2005	James Gallo
1973	Dean Bowyer	2006	Steven Chappell
1974	Guy Burgess		

1970: Rocky Mountain Rescue's emergency vehicle, a customized four-wheel-drive van. Also known as "the truck." "1970" is the radio number for the vehicle.

Anchor: A point to safely secure a rope, person, or any other object. Examples are large trees, big boulders, or climbing equipment secured in cracks in solid rock.

Avalanche beacon: A hand-sized device that is strapped to the body when one enters a snowslope that has some danger of avalanching. The device is a transceiver, i.e., it will transmit or receive depending on which mode it is set to. While in an avalanche zone, the beacon is set to transmit mode. If the person wearing the beacon is buried in an avalanche, others can set their beacons to receive and use them to zero in on the buried victim.

BASE jumpers: People who participate parachuting from ground-based objects such as **B**uildings, **A**ntennas, **S**pans or bridges, and **E**arth or cliffs.

Bash kit: A 35-pound pack full of anchor equipment, slings, carabiners, and miscellaneous hardware necessary to build anchors and technical rescue systems in the field.

Bean bag: A revolutionary body-splinting device, also called a vacuum splint. It is a mattress-like pad that fits the length of the litter. It is a thick plastic "bag" with a filler that gives it a similar consistency to that of a bean bag chair (thus the RMR-coined name). The bag is placed in the bottom of the litter, shaped to fit the body, and evacuated of air. It becomes a comfortable but rigid shell, stabilizing any broken bones in a similar but far superior way than a back board works.

Belay: The act of holding a rope for safety, tied to a person climbing or litter being lowered. The rope is held using an anchored friction device such as a brake plate. This allows easy control of a descent and will easily stop a falling climber.

Brake plate: A smooth, rectangular piece of metal with contoured slots cut on each side. Used to belay a litter or large load (greater than the weight of one person). Designed and built by RMR.

Bushwhack: Off-trail cross-country travel where one will whack or be whacked by bushes.

Cable kit: A pack filled with accessories for setting up a cable support system.

Cage: "The Cage" is a generic term for the RMR office and equipment storage room. The name is derived from the inner equipment bunker that had a lockable cage-like gate. Originally located in the basement of the University of Colorado Memorial Center.

CAP: Abbreviation for Civil Air Patrol, a nationwide organization responsible for locating ELT signals from downed aircraft.

Carabiner: A metal ring with a spring-loaded gate used by climbers to attach various climbing equipment together. Carabiners vary in shape and size, but are generally oval- or D-shaped and approximately the size of the palm of a hand. They attach climbing ropes to anchors, attach climbing harnesses to climbing ropes, attach slings to each other, etc.

Couloir: A channel or gulley that runs along the face of a mountain. When filled with snow, couloirs make excellent climbing and descent routes.

Crampon: Metal spikes attached to the bottom of a boot to assist in climbing steep snow or ice.

CSRB: Abbreviation for the Colorado Search and Rescue Board.

Crux: The most difficult spot on a climb. Most climbs or hikes have one most-difficult spot that determines the difficulty of the overall route.

DF: Abbreviation for direction finding. DF equipment is used in locating an emergency locater transmitter on a downed aircraft. DF equipment consists of a directional antenna and a specialized radio.

receiver. When used properly, the equipment will indicate direction and distance from the receiver to the transmitter.

ELT: Abbreviation for Emergency Locator Transmitter. An ELT is a radio beacon carried on most airplanes that is triggered during a crash. Direction-finding (DF) equipment can be used to help find the ELT and wreckage of the aircraft.

EMT: Abbreviation for emergency medical technician.

Evac: Short for "evacuation."

Flagging: A marker, usually a brightly colored piece of survey tape, that indicates the way to proceed on a route in the backcountry.

Fourteener: One of the 54 or so mountains or high points in Colorado that rises 14,000 feet above sea level.

Glissade: A method to rapidly descend a snowfield. It is a slide down the snow, usually controlled with an ice axe.

GPS: Abbreviation for global positioning system.

Hangfire: The upper edge of an avalanche run. It is the unstable area where the snow that has slid has broken away from snow remaining. It poses a threat to rescuers working in the avalanche debris area below.

Highline: The load-bearing cable or rope across a span as part of a tyrolean traverse system.

Ice axe: A tool to assist with climbing steep snow or ice. It is made of a long shaft with a specially designed head to grip snow or ice.

ICS: Abbreviation for Incident Command System.

Jet pack: RMR lingo for their fully self-contained backpackable oxygen systems, consisting of two approximately three-foot-long, fully pressurized steel oxygen cylinders, regulators, tubing, and face mask. The term reminds the rescuer carrying the pack into the field that if the valve of a cylinder happened to break due to dropping the pack, it would become a self-propelled rocket.

L-Per: A radio receiver used in direction finding. It displays radio signal strength and has a speaker that sounds the distinctive whine of an ELT signal.

LZ: Abbreviation for a helicopter landing zone.

MRA: Abbreviation for Mountain Rescue Association, founded in Seattle.

NTSB: Abbreviation for National Transportation Safety Board.

Packset: A term used for a handheld radio; a walkie-talkie.

PI: Abbreviation for poison ivy.

Probe line: A row of rescuers who systematically probe avalanche debris for buried victims. The line moves over the avalanche debris in a grid pattern, pushing 8- to 10-foot steel poles into the debris, looking for irregularities, digging up possible finds.

Prusik: Refers to a short cord tied in a loop, used to "grab on" to a rope. Used to hold people or equipment securely to a rope.

RP: Abbreviation for "reporting party," the person who initially reports an incident to emergency services, usually requesting a rescue.

SAR: Abbreviation for search and rescue.

Self-arrest: A technique to stop a slide on snow with an ice axe. The basic procedure is to put one's body in a stable sliding position and then dig the pick of the ice axe into the snow to create enough friction to stop the slide.

Sked: A "soft" litter, very useful for transport over snow surfaces.

Spiders: Rigging used to attach the Stokes litter to ropes for a vertical evac or to cable pulleys for a tyrolean traverse.

Tag line: A rope used to control the movement of a load (litter or person) on a tyrolean traverse.

Timberline: A well-defined altitude above which trees and large plants do not grow. The altitude varies with latitude and is approximately 11,500 feet above sea level in Colorado.

Tyrolean traverse: Also called a "tyrol" or highline traverse, it is a technique used to move a load (person, litter, equipment) over an obstacle, such as a stream, in a quick, efficient, and safe manner.

UTM: Acronym for Universal Transverse Mercator, a coordinate system used in navigation and available on maps and GPS receivers. UTM coordinates are measured in meters, giving a hiker a more intuitive estimate of distances than other map coordinate systems such as degrees, minutes, and seconds.

Vertical: In reference to an evac, a vertical-style evac. Involves two ropes and two litter bearers who descend a vertical face with the litter horizontal.

Wind chill: The effect of wind on the temperature of the body. The stronger the wind is, the lower the temperature of exposed body surface and clothing, thus turning cold weather into dangerously frigid weather.

Yagi: A type of antenna used in radio direction finding. The dimensions of the antennas used by RMR cause them to be directionally sensitive to ELT frequencies so that they can be pointed at the radio source.

About the Author

MARK SCOTT-NASH is a Colorado native and has been a member of Rocky Mountain Rescue since 1999. He has participated in more than 100 search-and-rescue missions and is trained as an emergency medical technician. Mark teaches mountaineering courses for the Colorado Mountain Club and has worked as a mountain guide on trips ranging from the Colorado mountains to the remote Himalayas. He has led more than a dozen expeditions to high peaks in Alaska, Canada, Argentina, Bolivia, Peru, and Nepal. Mark writes a regular mountaineering commentary column for the Boulder Daily Camera. He is an engineer by profession. Mark and his wife Shelly, a technical project manager, live in Boulder, Colorado.